Entrepreneur®
MAGAZINE'S

startup

Start Your Own

EVENT PLANNING BUSINESS

*Your Step-by-Step
Guide to Success*

Entrepreneur Press and Krist___ _____er

EP
Entrepreneur
Press

Editorial Director: Jere L. Calmes
Managing Editor: Marla Markman
Cover Design: Beth Hansen-Winter
Production: Eliot House Productions
Composition: Ed Stevens

Library of Congress Cataloging-in-Publication Data

Turner, Krista.
    Entrepreneur magazine's start your own event planning service / by Krista Thoren Turner.
        p.   cm.
    Includes index
    ISBN 1-932156-84-4
        1. Special events—Planning. 2. Business planning. I. Title: Start your own event planning service. II. Entrepreneur. III. Title.

GT3405.T87 2004
394.2'068--dc22   2004053213

Printed in Canada

09 08 07   10 9 8 7 6

Contents

Preface

Imagine the following scenario: You are out to dinner with the Smiths. They tell you that they want to throw an elaborate 21st birthday party for their daughter. They can afford to spend several hundred dollars, but because they have no spare time to organize the party, they need someone else to do it. Do you

a. run away screaming?

b. tell them that you really only do corporate events, but that you'd be happy to refer them to another planner?

c. grab a pen and ask them for more details?

d. beam at this happy coincidence and tell them that you've recently started such a business and would love to have them as customers?

If you answered a, you picked up this book by mistake. Put it down immediately! Reading it will only cause you pain, and that's what root canals are for.

If you answered b or c, we will take a wild guess that you already have an event planning business and perhaps also a specialization (e.g., corporate or social events). In either case, this book is for you, even if you're already well established. You'll find advice for expanding your client base, improving the service you provide, and maximizing your chances for continued success. You'll also find suggestions to help you fatten up your idea file (see Chapter 3).

If you answered d, however, we wish not only to assure you that this is definitely the book for you, but also to congratulate you for the courage and commitment you have shown in starting your own business.

This book covers all facets of event planning. Chapters 1, 2, and 3 provide background information about the event planning industry and what it takes to be a planner. In Chapters 4, 5, and 6, you'll learn what you need to know to get your own business up and running. These chapters cover everything from acquiring the necessary licenses to financing your business to hiring personnel. We even include sample documents. The final chapters (Chapters 7, 8, and 9) focus on making your business a success. We'll show you how to build a client base, promote your business, and manage your finances. You'll also learn how to avoid common industry pitfalls.

This book has two new kinds of tip boxes: Profile and Stat Fact. Profiles provides information about how a particular event planner handles some facet of the job. And Stat Fact lists interesting statistics about the event planning industry.

Our goal in writing this book is simple: We want you to know how to start an event planning business and how to keep improving it.

So grab a comfortable chair, and let's make plans.

Blueprint of
an Industry

Since you have opened the book to this page, you probably either have an event planning business or are considering starting one. In either case, read on as we take a general look at what event planners do and why they do it. Is event planning for you? We'll cover that, too. Finally, this chapter provides an overview of the special events industry and a sampling of ideas for conducting your own market research.

Questions, Always Questions

We begin by considering the *who, what, when, where, why*, and *how* of event planning (although not in that order). This discussion is introductory and general in nature. We will cover these *wh-* questions in more detail and with a different focus in Chapter 3.

What?

This question actually breaks down into two questions: *What* kinds of events are we talking about? *What* is event planning?

First things first: *What* kinds of events are we talking about? Generally speaking, special events occur for the following purposes:

- *Celebrations* (fairs, parades, weddings, reunions, birthdays, anniversaries)
- *Education* (conferences, meetings, graduations)
- *Promotions* (product launches, political rallies, fashion shows)
- *Commemorations* (memorials, civic events)

The above list is not an exhaustive one, but as the examples illustrate, special events may be business related, purely social, or somewhere in between. The advice in this book is relevant to the planning of all these types of events. Note that we will not focus on any one particular type of event. However, Entrepreneur's *Start Your Own Wedding Consultant Business* covers wedding planning in detail.

Now we move to the second *what* question: *What* is event planning?

Planners of an event may handle any or all of the following tasks related to that event:

- Conduct research
- Create an event design
- Find a site
- Arrange for food, decor, and entertainment
- Plan transportation to and from the event
- Send invitations to attendees
- Arrange any necessary accommodations for attendees
- Coordinate the activities of event personnel
- Supervise at the site
- Conduct evaluations of the event

How many of these activities your business engages in will depend on the size and type of a particular event, which will, in turn, depend on the specialization you choose. We will discuss all these tasks in Chapter 3. For details on specializing, see Chapter 2. For now, however, we continue on to the next question.

When Do Event Planners Work?

Few event planners, if any, have 9-to-5 jobs (unless, of course, they have a *day* job and conduct their event planning as a sideline; this strategy may be a good one if you are just starting out). By its very nature, event planning tends to involve evenings, weekends, holidays, and sometimes even specific seasons. How much time, and when, you must commit to working will depend, once again, on the specialization you choose.

Deborah K. Williams estimates she works 60 to 65 hours per week. She, Kim Quigley, and David Granger are all stockholders in Designs Behind the Scenes, their 13-year-old event planning company in Dallas. Their business is a combination of corporate and private events and rentals. October is their busiest month for corporate events, followed by December. They have private events most weekends.

Industry expert John Daly points out that summer is a slow period for corporate events. Also, by the second week in December, all the corporate holiday events are over.

As a general rule, social events involve more weekends and holidays than corporate events. Some areas of the country and some types of events have *on* and *off* seasons. However, no matter what your specialization (with the exception of parties for young children), you can count on working at least some evenings as you coordinate and supervise events. The planning of those events, however, will be done mostly during business hours.

Where Do Event Planners Work?

Some event planners work out of their homes, while others rent office space for their businesses. Each of these strategies has advantages and disadvantages. Chapter 4 details these pros and cons and provides information on choosing a location for your business.

Why Do People Hire Event Planners?

This question has a simple answer: Often individuals find that they lack the expertise and the time to plan events themselves. Independent planners can step in and give these events the attention they deserve.

Who Becomes an Event Planner?

Planners are often people who got their start in one particular aspect of special events. Martin Van Keken, of MVKA Productions in Vancouver, British Columbia, had a successful catering company before he decided to plan entire events. Initially, Lee J. Howard Entertainment Inc. in Atlanta provided entertainment only. Then, in response to client requests, Howard branched out. Many other planners have similar stories. This explains why planners often not only coordinate entire events, but may, in addition, provide one or more services for those events.

Profile

David Granger of Designs Behind the Scenes in Dallas works in both social and corporate markets. He finds that in a tougher economy, good customer service is critical. He says, "Clients are realizing that a beautiful party is not all that is required."

Often, owners of event planning businesses are also people who planned events for other companies before deciding to go into business for themselves. Joyce Barnes-Wolff planned in-house events for a retail chain for 11 years and then worked for another event planning company before starting JBW Productions in Columbus, Ohio. New York City planner Jaclyn Bernstein also planned events for another company before she and partner Robert Hulsmeyer bought it and turned it into Empire Force Events Inc.

Although the backgrounds of event planners may vary greatly, planners share many traits. Everyone we interviewed insisted that you have to have a passion for the event planning industry. Many said that they can't wait to get to the office most days. As industry expert Dr. Joe Goldblatt notes, "Successful event managers love their jobs."

John Daly, floral design specialist and industry expert, has written for industry publications, including *Special Events Magazine*. He also does a lot of public speaking. When he is asked about profits in the industry, he replies, "You have to get the passion, then the money will come. It's hard work. But it's rewarding if it's your passion."

Joyce Barnes-Wolff also stresses that people get into the event planning industry not because they want to get rich, but because they have a passion for it. "We all suffer from 'puppy syndrome,' " she says. "Clients love to throw us the ball and we'll run harder and faster every time they throw it and we'll jump over things. And all we want is for people to pat us on the head and say 'good job.' "

Growing Up Together

When Joyce Barnes-Wolff planned her first event, her task involved "... putting on a pot of coffee and calling the press and trying to get 25 people to show up." She learned and grew along with the retail company she worked for, and her last event for that company was a shareholders meeting for 18,000 people. After that, she planned events for a production company for about five years before starting her own business, JBW Productions. Although her company is now seven years old, she did not initially intend to strike out on her own. "I was handed a chunk of business," she says. Her local convention visitors bureau hired her directly to produce the Capitol Lights event. Since she began her business, her company has expanded to produce other corporate and nonprofit events.

What about the personality of event planners? When asked what traits are important in the industry, planners listed the following:

- *Organizational ability.* Everyone mentioned this trait. Therefore, be warned: If you would rather count every blade of grass on your lawn than make a list, this profession is not for you.

- *Attention to detail.* This is another must mentioned by most interviewees. Planners must think of, and keep track of, an amazing number of details. Planner Lee J. Howard suggests the following strategy, "Think from the completion of the result you want and then work backward to see how you can get there."

> ⚠️ **Beware!**
> Some of the anecdotes planners related convinced us that you would also be well advised to possess the following personality traits:
> ○ *A stout heart.* You can't be faint-hearted and be a successful planner. You are in charge of the entire event, and there are no second chances.
> ○ *Nerves of steel.* Glitches or no glitches, you must be upbeat and positive during the event. (You can cry and gnash your teeth later, in the car.)

Getting Philosophical

Event planners and industry experts have plenty of philosophies about their field and about their own roles in event planning. "Goodwill matters a lot in this business," says industry expert John Daly. "It's important to share knowledge." His motto? "Big fun is serious business."

"In this industry there is no right or wrong except to make the client happy," says David Granger.

Planners design events, hire personnel, and also contribute their own labor where needed. This multifaceted aspect of the profession explains Martin Van Keken's philosophy: "We're the architect, the contractor, and sometimes even the electrician," he says.

Joyce Barnes-Wolff views creative work as a major contribution her company makes to events. But creativity, she cautions, is not everything. "Without planning and follow-through, it's like a roof without a foundation," she says.

When asked about the qualities of successful event planners, Lee J. Howard has these succinct words: "Grace under pressure."

Jaclyn Bernstein knows exactly why event planners stick it out through pressure, crazy hours, and deadlines. "You have to love what you're doing," she says.

And, you may ask, what about a shared, industrywide philosophy? Is there a motto? You bet. "You're only as good as your last event."

- *Decision-making ability.* Anyone who is always the last of a group to order at a restaurant should consider a different industry. As an event planner, you will be called upon to make many decisions, sometimes in only a split second.

- *Good communication skills.* You'll need to convey your ideas and plans effectively to your clients, staff, and vendors, among others. You will need this ability not only as a sender, but also as a receiver of communication. Keep in mind that communication can be visual as well as verbal. Recognizing a blank look when you see one can enable you to clarify directions before some aspect of the event goes awry.

- *A liking for people.* This industry is very people-oriented. Jaclyn Bernstein mentioned a propensity for "taking care of people."

- *Creativity.* Whether you handle design elements of an event or not, creative talents are a definite plus. Furthermore, the definition of creativity may not always be what you think. "Creative is when you're on the job and Plan A isn't going to work and you have half an hour to figure out Plan B," says Patty Sachs, author of *Pick a Party Cookbook: The Big Book of Theme Party Refreshments and Table Décor,* among other books.

- *Flexibility.* "There's always something that will go differently than planned," says Martin Van Keken. "You've got to be ready." And you've got to be able to think on your feet.

- *Tact.* Sometimes you will have to break unhappy news to clients. For example, their budgets may not always be big enough to accomplish what they want. Also, they may want decor elements that either will not work well or are inappropriate. While these problems are less common when dealing with corporate clients, you will still find tact a necessary ingredient in successful business relationships.

> **Tip...**
>
> **Smart Tip**
>
> If you decide to volunteer, make sure you are not an "invisible" volunteer, one of the masses. Make sure you are assisting the person in charge and that you get experience with a large variety of

> **Bright Idea**
>
> Depending on the type of services they offer, independent planners might call themselves by any of the following titles: program manager, event planner, principal executive, fundraising consultant, meeting consultant, or event coordinator, among others.

If you have most of these traits, event planning may be a good profession for you. How do you find out for sure? "Volunteer, volunteer, volunteer!" says Sachs. "Offer to assist the chairperson of a large fundraising event, the bigger the better.

Follow that person through from start to finish, sitting in on all meetings and pushing the event over the hill, grunt work included. This will establish the area of planning that you find most appealing and for which you are most suited." If you already have some idea of which types of events you'd like to plan, make sure you concentrate your volunteer efforts there.

How Do Event Planners Do It?

The answer to this question is what this book, as well as your own experience, will show you. So pull up a comfortable chair and read on. Our first step will be to examine the event planning industry itself.

A History Lesson

The special events industry has grown enormously in the last two decades. According to recent research conducted by Dr. Joe Goldblatt, CSEP (Certified Special Events Professional), annual spending for special events worldwide is estimated at $500 billion. Goldblatt is the founder of ISES (International Special Events Society) and the founding director of the Event Management Program at George Washington University. Currently at Johnson and Wales University, he is the dean of the Alan Shawn Feinstein Graduate School, which offers the first MBA concentration in Event Leadership. According to Goldblatt, in spite of recent challenges, such as a poor economy and an increased terrorism alert, profits in this industry remain solid. "Gross profit margins vary greatly but are usually in the 30 to 40 percent range. Starting salaries are usually in the high $20s, and, according to a study I conducted, over 55 percent of all event planners earn between $55,000 and $100,000 per year."

A recent article in *Special Events Magazine* reports that the majority of event professionals believe the downturn of the past couple of years is in large part the trough of a normal business cycle.

> **Bright Idea**
>
> When a company holds a meeting in a major city and the attendees travel to the meeting from other cities or states, a planner may use a destination manager's services to take care of the attendees' needs at their meeting location. Destination managers coordinate and supervise meetings in their cities, transport attendees to and from their hotels and airports, and take attendees on tours to give them a feel for the cities they are visiting. Jaclyn Bernstein, president of Empire Force Events Inc. in New York City, handles a lot of destination management business.

Most see unique opportunities ahead. *Meetings & Conventions* magazine, a leading source for the meetings industry, reports that the meetings market held steady, despite challenges.

Goldblatt adds that although the corporate events market may make only a slow recovery, the social events market is booming. "As the baby boomers age, they have more to celebrate—and do! Seventy million Americans are turning 50 in the next seven years, and they will not do this quietly."

Sachs agrees, "The event, party, and celebration industry is growing more each year, in a steady way." Like Goldblatt, she points out the large number of baby boomers celebrating milestone birthdays. In addition, she says, many are now celebrating landmark anniversaries or their offspring's graduations and weddings. "To top all of this, these baby boomers are often owners or executives in businesses that were established some 25 years ago, which brings about many corporate celebrations."

Although potential profits, especially in social event planning, are substantial, keep in mind that it takes the average event planning business two to three years to make a healthy profit. Why? One reason is that most clients come from word-of-mouth referrals, and it can take a while before a solid base of contacts is developed. For detailed information on building a solid client base, see Chapter 7.

Going Glam

Along with increased demand for special events, and perhaps because of it, the industry has become much more sophisticated. According to Daly, "It's become a force to be reckoned with." Twenty years ago, he says, a party was a tablecloth and a centerpiece. Event planners were not taken seriously. When he told people he created parties for a living, he remembers, it was laughable. "Now it's interesting," he says.

David Granger, a veteran in the industry, concurs. "People know what they are looking for," he says. "A certain quality is expected now."

Joyce Barnes-Wolff makes a similar point: "There is more credibility than . . . when event specialists were the people who did country club parties." Now, she adds, huge concerns like Disney, Radio City Music Hall, Universal Studios, Paramount, and others have become involved in the special events industry.

To Market, To Market

Broadly speaking, there are two markets for event planning services: corporate and social. Market information is more readily available for corporate meetings than for other events, but we will attempt to give you a good idea of both markets.

The Corporate Market

We will use the term *corporate* to include not only companies but also charities and non-profit organizations. All these entities use special events to reach their target markets and to increase their visibility in the community. In fact, special events have become increasingly important as competition forces organizations to look for new ways to get their messages across to consumers or contributors.

Charities and nonprofit organizations host gala fundraisers, receptions, and athletic competitions, among other events, to expand their public support base and raise the funds they require. Such organizations find that special events are cost-effective and have a high impact. Thousands of these events occur each year, and although the large ones require specialized event planning experience, you may find smaller local events to plan.

Companies host trade shows, conventions, company picnics, holiday parties, and meetings for staff members, board members, or stockholders. There is a huge market for these types of events. In one year alone, the total number of meetings held in the United States was over 1 million, according to *Meetings Market Report* conducted for *Meetings & Conventions* magazine.

Whether you plan meetings, fundraisers, or receptions, there are opportunities available in corporate event planning. But according to expert John Daly, corporate events currently involve "less spending, less travel, less opulence. Clients want to see a return on their investments more than ever before." Patty Sachs, author of party-planning books and newsletters, says that corporations want events that are original and striking enough to be long remembered: "Themes are extremely popular." So are unusual sites, customized entertainment, and an increased degree of guest involvement.

Planning corporate events can provide you with a steady, profitable amount of business, but if you are a beginning event planner, Daly recommends that you begin by planning social events.

Stat Fact
According to a recent *Meetings Outlook Survey* conducted jointly by Meeting Professionals International (MPI) and the American Society of Association Executives (ASAE), the average successful independent meeting planner specializing in the corporate market will arrange approximately 47 meetings per year.

Stat Fact
The *Meetings Market Report* is conducted every two years and published in *Meetings & Conventions* magazine, a leading source for the meetings industry. A recent report indicates that in one year alone, there were more than 1 million meetings. The same report shows that companies and organizations spent $40.8 billion on meetings in that same year.

The Social Market

Social events include weddings, birthdays, anniversary parties, bar and bat mitzvahs, Sweet 16 parties, children's parties, reunions, etc. You may decide to handle all these events or to specialize in one or more of them.

Most people who employ event planners for these types of parties are in the middle- to upper-income levels and have some spare income but no spare time. Such clients are likely to live in affluent suburbs. Typically, these clients have household incomes of at least $60,000.

The market for social events, especially birthdays and anniversaries, is expected to continue to increase over the next few years, as baby boomers mature. This group has children getting married, parents celebrating golden anniversaries, and their own silver wedding anniversaries to celebrate. Industry experts agree that baby boomers will be a major source of income for event planning entrepreneurs in the coming years.

Scoping It Out

Many interviewees told us that their market research was very informal in nature, consisting of knowledge gained through years of involvement in the industry. Deborah Williams, Kim Quigley, and David Granger all have years of experience in the event planning or supply industry. Their target market is the Dallas-Ft. Worth area. However, they also operate nationally, producing corporate events in Florida, Oklahoma, and Ohio. Most of their clients come to them through organizations they belong to or because they have been involved in the industry for many years. "So you know the resources and the people," Quigley says.

If you already have experience in event planning or a related industry, you may be starting your own business partly because discussions with colleagues make you aware that a need exists. This kind of knowledge is valuable, but Goldblatt points out that competition is now global as well as local, and all event planners should do market research. With this idea in mind, we now offer some suggestions on how to conduct this type of research. For a more thorough treatment of the topic, consult Chapter 1, "Conducting Market Research," in *Start-Up Basics*.

Conduct a Market Analysis

One of your first tasks is to determine the market limits or trading area of your business. These limits will vary depending upon the type of event planning service you offer. For example, if you plan parties, you may limit your market to your county. If you plan corporate meetings, however, you may have a national client base.

Studies show that a population base of at least 50,000 is needed to support an event planning service. Keep in mind that the higher the income level of that population, the more potential clients there will be for your business.

Stat Fact

The Meeting Professional, the magazine published by Meeting Professionals International, reports that the average salary for independent planners is $60,230.

Your first step should be to conduct a market analysis. Find out the answer to the following questions:

- Is the population base large enough to support your event planning service?
- Does the community have a stable economic base that will provide a healthy environment for your business?
- Are the area's demographic characteristics compatible with the market you wish to serve?

Many chambers of commerce have offices that track their area's economic development. These offices are usually called either Office of Economic Development or Economic Development Council. Find an office in your area, and look for the above information. In addition, look at reports and studies conducted by trade associations. You can also contact the Census Bureau by e-mail at webmaster@census.gov or by mail at Customer Services, U.S. Census Bureau, 4700 Silver Hill Rd., Washington,

Free Association

Actually, they usually aren't free, but memberships in industry-related associations can be well worth the investment. Associations usually offer networking opportunities and a wealth of industry-specific information, such as market statistics, member lists, books, and reference materials. They may also offer discounts on purchases from certain suppliers.

Before you join an association, think about why you are joining. Is it to gain education or access to information? Is it for networking opportunities? Is it to enhance your credibility? Whatever the reason, use your association as a resource. It is worth the money only if you take advantage of the benefits membership offers.

There are several associations specific to the event planning industry, including the International Special Events Society and Meeting Professionals International. For information on contacting an industry association, please see the Appendix at the end of this guide.

DC 20233. Its Web site is www.census.gov, and the call center is also available at (301) 763-4636.

If you'll be planning corporate events, you also need to know the number of corporations in your service area that hold regular conventions and meetings, the size of these companies, their budgets for these events, and if they are using outside services.

Interview Prospective Clients

The next step is to interview prospective clients. What are their needs? How likely are they to use a service like yours? If you are planning corporate events, interview meeting planners and directors of marketing and public relations, as well as event directors at convention halls and hotels. If your business will focus on social events, interview women in affluent households (studies show women do most social planning). Whatever your specialization, also consider interviewing professionals in related fields. Photographers and caterers know a lot about the nature of the special events occurring in the area. You can survey your targeted market by direct mail, by telephone, or in person.

Next, Goldblatt suggests, try to get a few clients. "If people are not willing to pay you, they're not fully committed," he says.

Stat Fact
The Bureau of Labor Statistics publishes the *Consumer Expenditure Survey* (CES). To learn how families and individuals spend their money, order a copy of the latest CES. Call (202) 691-5200 or write to the Bureau of Labor Statistics, Division of Information Services, 2 Massachusetts Ave. NE, Room 2860, Washington, DC 20212. This information can also be ordered from the Bureau of Labor Statistics' Web site at www.dol.gov or http://stats.bls.gov.

Analyze the Competition

Competition in the event planning market is fierce, but it is not insurmountable. If you are targeting the corporate market, your competition will consist not only of other event planning entrepreneurs, but also of in-house meeting planners hired by corporations. However, with recent trends in corporate downsizing, many companies are looking to outsource these responsibilities to keep costs low. You may be able to assess the competition by asking corporations about the planners they work with.

Bright Idea
To help size up the competition, go to as many special events as possible and find out who planned them. Take note of details of the event. Consider videotaping, if permitted. Your goal is to learn everything you can.

Trade associations such as ISES or MPI may not be able to disclose members' names, but they might be willing to tell you how many of their members are located in your area.

In the social arena, your main competition will be other event planning entrepreneurs, as well as some caterers, florists, etc., who have taken on the responsibilities of planning events as a sideline function. Most of the competition you'll face will be local; try checking in your phone book under Event Planners or Party Planners to see how many others there are. Be aware, however, that many event planners do not buy advertising, preferring to rely solely on word-of-mouth to do their advertising for them. This means you may have to get creative to figure out how much local competition you face. Ask vendors which planners they work with. Go to party supply stores and see if you can find out who their major customers are. Ask all your questions face-to-face, rather than by phone. If you are friendly and explain that you are trying to figure out if there is enough demand for another planning business, most people will cooperate.

If you find a large amount of competition in your area, don't be discouraged. Instead, look for a niche you can fill (see Chapter 2). As we have stressed in this chapter, social event planning is the ideal sector in which to begin your career. Social planning is a growth industry—there are more opportunities out there than those planners in the marketplace can handle. Also realize that these competitors may not provide the quality, service, or expertise you plan to. They may not market themselves as effectively as you will. In a service industry, there will always be room for someone who can provide excellent service at reasonable prices. If you strive to be the best, research your market, promote yourself, and develop a good business plan, you will find your spot in the marketplace. In the next chapter, we focus on maximizing your chances for success.

Beware!

During economic slowdowns, clients are increasingly budget-conscious and short on time. Yet clients have also become more sophisticated. Both corporate and social clients look for a maximum return on investment and are wary of committing themselves early to events. You'll find that as an event planner, you face a variety of challenges, including high expectations, tight budgets, and short lead times.

Profile

Dallas planner Kim Quigley says she spends most of her time on vendor consultations, networking, bookkeeping, and event design. However, she also conducts on-site supervision, consults with clients, and routes deliveries to event venues. She goes to staff meetings once a week and travels about three times a year.

Getting There from Here— Laying the Groundwork

Now that you've decided event planning looks interesting and you have the right personality characteristics to do the job, it's time to name your business and hang out your shingle, right? Wrong. Before you do anything else, take the following four steps:

▲

1. Research the industry.
2. Find your niche.
3. Determine your start-up costs.
4. Create a map for success.

This chapter gives you the basic tools to accomplish these tasks.

Researching the Industry

Some aspects of event planning are much more complicated than many entrepreneurs realize. The delicacies of developing solid vendor relations, establishing good rapport with clients, and heading off potential problems before they affect your event (and therefore your reputation) can only be conquered by extensive study and experience.

You've taken a big step by purchasing this guide, which covers the nuts and bolts of all aspects of event planning. We'll help you research your market and find a niche that's right for you. We'll show you how you can promote yourself and your business until you develop a solid base of clients and potential customers. We'll warn you of potential pitfalls and show you how to ward them off before your business falls victim to them.

Even so, your research shouldn't stop here. You should also do the following:

Making the Grade

Consider getting a degree or certificate from a local university in event planning or management. According to industry expert Dr. Joe Goldblatt, 300 colleges and universities offer classes in event management. A list of the institutions offering educational opportunities in this field is available from Meeting Professionals International (MPI). (See the Appendix for contact information.)

Also consider working to become a CSEP (Certified Special Events Professional) or CMP (Certified Meeting Planner). These designations are given out by ISES (International Special Events Society) and MPI, respectively. Many corporations, and some members of the general public, look for these designations when hiring planners. Because of the research and study it takes to become a CMP or CSEP, clients know that these planners are professionals.

- *Conduct the market research as suggested in this guide.* There is no substitute for doing your homework.
- *Network with other event planning entrepreneurs and business owners by joining local associations.* Industry ties are crucial in the event planning business.
- *Contact the national associations for the latest in research and practice guidelines,* as well as for any other help they can provide. You can find the relevant contact information in the Appendix.
- *Keep up with industry trends through business journals and other publications.* These are valuable resources.
- *Read everything you can find on the event planning industry.* This includes newspaper articles.
- *Volunteer your time to a local charity event.* Not only will you get hands-on experience, but you will make valuable contacts that will help you down the road.

> ## Profile
> Event planner David Granger handles a variety of events, both corporate and social. Recently he has expanded his services to include bar and bat mitzvahs. However, he has many years of experience with large events. "I do dinner parties and events for hotels, with buffet tables, special effects, and entertainment."

Finding Your Niche

We've already mentioned the fact that most event professionals focus on either corporate or social events. However, you should consider specializing even further, narrowing your attention to children's parties, corporate retreats, or other types of events. Why? "Without a niche market, it makes it hard for the market to find you," says Dr. Joe Goldblatt, industry expert and founder of ISES. For example, if you're known as your community's expert on anniversary parties, a client wanting to throw such a party is more likely to come to you than to a general party planner.

Specializing in one or two types of events will also make your job easier. You can become an expert in one type of event faster than you can in multiple events. Specializing will save you time because you'll soon be familiar with all the elements of, and vendors required for, the type of event you choose. And as an event professional, time is one of your most valuable resources—the more you can save, the better.

Specialize!

This said, what are your options for specializing? They are limited only by your imagination. Industry expert, consultant, and author Patty Sachs agrees that specializing is a good way to establish yourself in the industry. She suggests the following possible niches for social event planners:

- Hospitality suites (events held in the "party" room of a retirement home or a business)
- Parties away from home (events hosted by hotel guests)
- Surprise parties
- Progressive parties (events at more than one venue, usually involving transportation from one location to another—e.g., tours, scavenger hunts)
- His 'n' hers showers (wedding and baby)
- 1-year-old birthday parties
- Theme parties
- "Golden" parties (50th anniversaries, 50th birthdays, etc.)
- Milestone birthdays
- Weekend event guest services (events to entertain out-of-town guests over the weekend—e.g., tours, barbecues)
- Kids' parties
- Kids' event areas for grown-up parties

The niches listed above all have a social focus, even though your client might also be a corporation. Below we list some additional possibilities for finding your niche in business-related events.

- Mall events (fashion shows, store grand openings, department-store promotions)
- Meetings and conferences
- Awards events
- Fundraisers
- Corporate retreats or picnics

If you do decide to focus on one type of event, be sure that your market area has enough of a demand, as discussed in Chapter 1. Also, make sure that you leave room for adding other types of events by not choosing too specific a business name (see Chapter 4).

Profile

Industry expert John Daly, CSEP, started his first event planning company in the mid-'70s on $4,000. He drove an old van, which he parked out of sight. His first location was a 250-square-foot workroom in Los Angeles. He spent the majority of his start-up money on two suits. "I wanted to look successful," he explains. "It worked." Within four years he had 35 full-time employees and a fleet of cars. "I was at the right place at the right time."

Bright Idea

You could specialize in "current events" parties. For example, what about that famous art exhibit coming to town? Get your props together and go for a museum look to create an unusual party. And don't forget special dates, anniversaries, and other time-related themes (e.g., millennium, anniversary of space flight, etc.).

Determining Your Start-Up Costs

How much money will you need to start your event planning business? That will depend on the cost of living in the area your business serves and whether you work from home or rent office space. It will also depend on your own taste and lifestyle choices.

Keep in mind that while working from home will keep your costs low, you cannot start any but the smallest event planning business on a shoestring. At a minimum, you must buy equipment and a good insurance policy. You may also need advertising. All these expenses can be costly. The start-up worksheet on page 21 should give you an indication of how much money you will need to start your event planning service. Fill in the column labeled "My Own" with your own estimated costs.

This chart lists the start-up costs for two hypothetical event planning services. The first business is homebased with no permanent employees. The owner already

Special Delivery

Most planners we interviewed specialized in either social or corporate events, with little mixing of the two types. Which of these you choose (or whether you choose to mix them) will depend on several factors:

○ *Amount of experience.* Industry expert John Daly points out that corporations are extremely sophisticated. If you are just starting out in the industry, he recommends beginning with private events. "You have to get seasoned before you do corporate [events]."

○ *Personality.* Clients tend to have more invested, emotionally, in social events. Generally speaking, social event planning requires even greater amounts of patience and tact than does corporate event planning.

○ *Lifestyle preference.* Consider what you expect as time off and whether you have strong feelings about the time of year you'd like to vacation. Everyone interviewed mentioned that they work long hours, well over 40 per week. "Private parties take a lot more time than corporate events. They're much more demanding," says Daly. This is partly because of the client's emotional investment in the event. Working during holidays is a virtual certainty if you do social parties. Furthermore, specializing in wedding anniversary parties might have you heavily booked in the spring and gasping for work the rest of the year. A corporate specialization, on the other hand, may involve more travel.

has a basic computer and modem and some office furniture. She used her start-up money to buy liability insurance, event-planning software, a better cell phone, a digital camera, and a multifunction printer/copier/fax machine. She also established a Web site and paid a graphic design student to produce a high-quality business card and letterhead logo. She started her business on a shoestring.

Beware!
Remember, if you live in an area where the cost of living is especially high, most (but not all) of your costs will be higher. Make sure you do in-depth researching of the costs you can expect to incur.

The higher end business occupies 1,000 square feet of office space. The owner/manager of this business employs a full-time junior planner and a part-time bookkeeper, as well as temporary employees who handle clerical work and who may help prepare for various events. This owner upgraded her existing computer equipment, bought office furniture and cell phones for herself and her assistant, added a phone line and a Web site, bought several types of insurance, and invested in business cards, stationery, and an ad in the Yellow Pages.

Both owners will derive their income from pre-tax net profit. Annually, these new businesses will gross $85,000 and $250,000, respectively. The start-up table lists pre-opening costs for the businesses.

Creating a Map for Success

To make sure you keep your business goals and strategies clearly in sight, you need the following two items:

1. a business plan
2. a mission statement

Your Business Plan

Broadly speaking, your business plan should discuss the event planning industry, your business structure, the service you will offer, your clients, the competition and how you will beat it, your income and cash flow, and other relevant financial information.

A well-conceived business plan will provide you with a map for the future of your venture, as well as something by which to gauge your

Profile
Deborah Williams says she and Kim Quigley spent $5,000 in 1990 to start Designs Behind the Scenes. They bought basic office equipment, including a computer and fax machine. They also invested in distinctive, high-quality business cards.

progress. Your plan thus becomes an operating tool that will help you manage your business. In addition, a business plan is the chief instrument you will use to communicate your ideas to others—including businesspeople, bankers, and partners. If you seek financing for your business, the plan will become the basis for your loan proposal. For in-depth instructions on creating your business plan, see Chapter 3, "Business Plan," in *Start-Up Basics*.

Your Mission Statement

Your mission statement is also a crucial part of giving your business every chance for success. Quite simply, a mission statement identifies, in a few sentences, your company's goals. Construct your company's mission statement by asking yourself the following questions:

- What kind of service do I want my company to provide for clients?
- What role will my company play in the event planning industry?
- What are my goals for my company's future?

Now that you have some of the basic tools you need to start your business, it's time to get down to the nitty-gritty of planning an event. Get ready to have some fun!

Start-Up Expenses

Start-Up Expenses	Low	High	My Own
Rent/security deposit	$0	$2,300	
Equipment	$5,000	$17,000	
Inventory	$0	$500	
Licenses and taxes	$250	$350	
Communications	$100	$250	
Payroll	$0	$4,000	
Advertising/promotion	$500	$2,000	
Legal fees and accounting	$650	$1,500	
Insurance (first quarter)	$800	$1,700	
Miscellaneous	$750	$1,500	
Total	$8,050	$31,1000	

3

A Day in the Life

This chapter covers the nuts and bolts of planning an event. We will take you through the steps involved and give you helpful hints along the way.

Dr. Joe Goldblatt, CSEP, has identified what he calls the Five Phases of Event Management: research, design, planning, coordination, and evaluation. His focus is on the production of large-scale events, and he has written several books on the topic (see the Appendix). Here we borrow his framework and adapt it to include the production of smaller events, with one vocabulary change. Because we use the term *planning* in this book to talk about the overall activity that includes these five phases, we will avoid confusion by referring to this phase as organization.

Research

The best way to reduce risk (whatever the kind) is to do your homework. For large events, research may mean making sure that there is a demand for the event. To find out this kind of information, you can conduct surveys or interviews, or you can assemble small groups of potential attendees, called focus groups, for discussion. Although you are researching demand for an event instead of demand for your business, the strategies are the same as those discussed in the market research sections in Chapter 1 of this book and in Chapter 1, "Conducting Market Research," in *Start-Up Basics*.

Tip...

Smart Tip

If you have to nix a client's suggestion, be tactful. Also, it's a good idea to have a countersuggestion handy. People usually accept the rejection of their idea or request much better if they are provided with an alternative rather than a flat "not pos-

If you are new to the event planning industry, research may mean finding out all you can about vendors and suppliers. As you meet with potential vendors, note which events they specialize in and how much they charge. Even if you decide during the

On the Road

If the event will be held in another city, the local convention and visitors bureau should be able to help you. It can guide you to a hotel that meets your client's needs and stays within your budget. These bureaus should also have a great deal of information on local attractions and sites for meetings and conventions. Convention personnel in hotels can offer valuable suggestions, but remember that they may have their own agenda. If you intend to look for suppliers or vendors in a city you have never visited, ask for referrals from other planners who have worked there. They may be able to direct you to excellent providers.

interview that you won't use their services right away, you should still take notes for future reference. Industry expert, author, and consultant Patty Sachs recommends using small cards and filing them in a box divided into main-event supplier categories. She cautions owners to note prices, style numbers, lead time, contact persons, and anything else that seems pertinent, even if you don't use the vendor for that particular event. "You are as good as your Rolodex," she advises. You could also list this information on your computer if you prefer. For more information on hiring vendors, see Chapter 6.

Profile
Joyce Barnes-Wolff of JBW Productions in Ohio keeps a drawer of new ideas. "Look at movies, music, what people are doing, what's hot." Wherever she goes and whatever she's doing, one little corner of her mind is always idea-gathering. "I can't shut it off," she says.

Research also may mean talking to other planners who have produced events similar to the one on which you are working. Or you may find yourself reading up on issues of custom and etiquette, especially if you are unfamiliar with a particular type of event.

Whatever kind of event you are planning, research should include asking your client a lot of questions *and writing down the answers.* New York City planner Jaclyn Bernstein, DMCP (Destination Management Certified Professional), works primarily with clients from out of town. To avoid communication problems, she makes sure she knows what the client's goals are and how the client thinks the event should be handled. "Try to use the client's exact words in your proposal," she suggests.

Always find out what customers hope to accomplish with an event. Do they want to introduce a new product, motivate employees, or provide a forum for networking? Do they want to put together a spectacular college reunion? Do they want to celebrate their parents' anniversary with an unforgettable party? Clients may want an event that is strictly business, strictly social, or somewhere in between.

Interviewing a client may not be what you immediately think of as research. However, asking too few questions or not listening adequately to a client's answers, can compromise the success of the event you plan. You must find out the answers to "reporter" questions similar to the ones addressed in Chapter 1:

Bright Idea
Most people love surprises, so include some in your event design. These can range from small surprises (inexpensive gifts given to each child in attendance) to larger ones (unexpected special effects). One cautionary note, however. If you plan a surprise party, make sure that it does not involve surprising the guest of honor at his or her home. This strategy can result in embarrassment for everyone!

- *Who?* Who are the attendees, and how many of them will be at the event (a dozen company executives, 30 children, 80 elderly ping-pong enthusiasts)?

- *What?* What kind of event will this be (a family reunion, an elegant sit-down banquet, a fashionable but laid-back art show reception)? Don't forget to ask about the style of the event (formal, relaxed, traditional, avant garde, etc.) and whether your client wants a theme event (see discussion below).

- *When?* Find out the date of the event.

- *Where?* The client may want you to suggest a venue for the event, but you should always find out what type of location is desired (something unusual, informal, elegant? indoors or outdoors?).

- *Why?* Find out the reason for the event. What is the client's goal or objective? (See earlier discussion.)

- *How?* How does the client want guests to remember the event? As the most original picnic they've ever been to? As

> ## Smart Tip
> Tip...
>
> Always give attendees a deadline for responding to announcements if they must confirm attendance. This will ensure that you meet your own deadlines. If you fail to conclude arrangements for airfare or hotel rooms in time, you will lose discounts offered for advance reservations.

By Invitation Only

Any invitations you send potential attendees should include the following information:

- ❍ Event
- ❍ Host's name
- ❍ Date
- ❍ Time
- ❍ Location
- ❍ RSVP phone number

Optional elements include the following:

- ❍ Significance of the event (purpose, frequency, historic importance)
- ❍ Dress requirements
- ❍ Directions and parking instructions
- ❍ Names of prominent speakers
- ❍ VIP status
- ❍ Complimentary ticket enclosure

a holiday evening filled with one surprise after another? As a company party with the best food they've had in a long time? The issue of how guests should remember an occasion is crucial in deciding which aspects of the event should be given priority. Recognizing that few clients have unlimited funds, always find out what aspects of the event your customer feels are most important.

Smart and Trendy

Several current trends have influenced either the types of events held or the planning of events. Most notable are the following trends:

Event Trends

- ○ *Streamlined events.* The emphasis is on doing more with less and on working smarter. In troubled economic times, even corporations scale back their events.
- ○ *Heritage-related events.* Festivals of all kinds are still extremely popular.
- ○ *Local events:* Companies are doing what they can to reduce the need for travel. Instead of one large national event, some corporations now hold several regional events.
- ○ *"Recycled" events.* There has been a recent increase in party-pooling (i.e., two or more hosts combining their resources to produce an event) and repeat parties (i.e., reusing decor for another party the following day).

Planning Trends

- ○ *Concern for charities.* Recently, organizers of social events (e.g., birthday parties) have requested guest donations to charity in lieu of gifts. Both corporations and individuals often donate leftover food to local homeless shelters and food banks.
- ○ *Accessibility for the disabled.* The Americans with Disabilities Act requires that all publicly accessible buildings accommodate disabled people. Many planners go even beyond what is now required by law.
- ○ *Concern for the environment.* When possible, planners are using recyclable products for their events, providing recycling bins, and using glass and china instead of paper and Styrofoam products.
- ○ *Healthful eating.* Caterers and event planners alike are taking notice of dietary concerns. Whether it be vegetarian, low-fat, Kosher, or low-carb dishes, most caterers can accommodate these needs. Confer with your clients before planning any menus to see what, if any, special meals they would like to provide.
- ○ *Responsible drinking.* This trend has resulted in decreased amounts of alcohol at events and in the provision of designated drivers.

And, unlike a reporter, you must always add the crucial additional question:

- *How much?* In other words, what is the available budget? This piece of information will greatly affect your design of the event, because many ideas (yours or the client's) will not be possible to achieve with the funds available. Telling clients that what they want is impossible given their budget is not a job for the faint-hearted. On the other hand, remember that anyone who chooses to plan events is both stouthearted

and has nerves made of steel (see Chapter 1), *so you can do it*. Just make sure you are tactful so that the client won't run off, never to knock at your door again.

Once you have noted answers to the basic seven questions, you need more specific information. Do your clients want to have any live entertainment at the event? What kind? What type of food and beverages would they like? How elaborate must the props or decorations be? Do they want a photographer or videographer? Will transportation be needed? Should there be valet parking?

Add these details to your notebook. Or make copies of the Event Design Worksheet, starting on page 36, and fill one out for each event.

Adequate research is important to the success of any event you plan. Yet Goldblatt finds that the research phase often does not receive enough attention. Make sure you have asked and received answers to all the above questions before you proceed to the design phase.

Design

Your creativity comes most into play in the design phase of event planning, during which you sketch out the overall feel and look of the event. This is the time to brainstorm, either by yourself or with your employees. It's also the time to pull out and look through your idea file. (You do have one, don't you? If not, read on and take notes.) Don't forget to consult your notebook for the client's answers to the

Bright Idea

As a first step in social event planning, consultant Patty Sachs suggests providing every potential client with a sheet that briefly details how your company works, what the general price structure is like, etc. This strategy ensures that clients are aware you'll require a deposit and that your company does not produce events for $10 per hour!

Smart Tip

It is a good idea not to give the client more than an overall sketch of the event design until the contract is signed. Otherwise you risk giving away the results of your creative labor for next to nothing.

questions you asked in the research phase. These responses, especially the one regarding the event budget, will help you to thoroughly check each idea for feasibility, preferably before suggesting it to the client.

Get the Idea

Sachs has the following suggestions for ensuring you are never stumped for design ideas to build on. "Attend openings, promotions, shows, and other events to study the way that they are produced," she says. "Save invitations and programs. Make 'event idea' cards, and file them in a box according to category."

> **Bright Idea**
>
> If you are planning a theme event, you can get great ideas by renting movies set in the appropriate time period or location. And don't forget other media possibilities (e.g., magazines).

If you are stumped for ideas to propose to your client, consider a theme event. Although no longer as novel as they were a few years ago, they are still popular. Themes may be inspired by a variety of factors, including time (Roaring '20s, Medieval festival), place (Caribbean Island, outer space), hobbies (Night at the Theater, Spa Party), or special events (Indy 500, Academy Awards).

Going in Style

The design phase is the time to pay close attention to the style of the event. If the client wants an elegant banquet with Victorian accents, sites like a giant hayloft or a space museum aren't good bets. (Yes, we know that's an extreme example, but you get the point.) On the other hand, a boating party followed by an open-air picnic, while not the first type of event that springs to mind, might work extremely well if the site, decor, catering, and entertainment fit the style of the event. The rest of our discussion of the design phase will focus on these four aspects of the event.

1. *Site.* Your choice of site will depend on several factors. Chief among these are your client, the event budget, and the purpose of the event. Corporate events, meetings, and conventions typically take place in hotels, convention centers, meeting centers, clients' facilities, or restaurants. More elaborate corporate events may take place at exotic sites, such as on cruise ships or in resorts.

   Social events can be held virtually anywhere your imagination (or your client's) will go. Possible event sites include the following:
   - *Fresh air* (garden or park, farm or ranch, forest or meadow)
   - *On the move* (ship or yacht, train, double-decker bus, trolley)
   - *Home, sweet home* (house, mansion, castle)
   - *Child's play* (zoo, theme park, children's restaurant, circus)

▲

- *Cultured pearls* (university, museum, planetarium, symphony hall)
- *Good sports* (swimming pool, miniature golf course, baseball diamond, skating rink)

Be aware that site choice can dictate other aspects of an event because sites sometimes have regulations regarding type of decor, the number of guests allowed, whether alcohol may be served, etc. If the site is outdoors, you'll need to make provisions for electricity, water, and restroom facilities, as well as for shelter from inclement weather.

When looking at sites, remember that price is one of many factors to consider. Look at the entire package of amenities and services offered. Make sure you understand what is included in price quotes. Some sites include taxes and service charges in their quotes while others do not. Keep in mind that a site with a low-end quote may turn out to be more expensive than one with a high-end quote if the former charges for services the latter offers for free. Carefully compare services and prices. Consultant Patty Sachs offers an additional piece of advice, "Get the reactions of others who have rented the site for events."

2. *Decor.* Creativity is a key element in this aspect of event planning. For this reason, the decor margin of profit can be as much as 40 percent for a large, elaborate event. If you are handling the decor yourself, remember to allow for the creative work involved. Do not give clients estimates until you are sure of what they want and how much time and effort you will spend to achieve it. "Clients always want a price before they've defined what the creative demand is," warns Joyce Barnes-Wolff.

Keep in Mind

Do not forget the Americans with Disabilities Act. As mentioned above, all buildings with public access must accommodate disabled people. Keep special needs in mind when selecting sites or designing room layouts, especially for large events. Look for the following:

- ○ Wheelchair space
- ○ Ramps
- ○ Handrails
- ○ A clear line of sight between audience and sign-language interpreter
- ○ Appropriate table heights

For more information, call the Americans with Disabilities Act information line: (800) 514-0301.

Decor elements can include, but are not limited to, the following:

- *Constructed set elements* (castle, bridge, storefront)
- *Painted backdrops* (mural, play scenery)
- *Props* (fountain, trellis, palm trees, furniture)
- *Fabric displays* (swags, drapings)
- *Floral treatments* (centerpieces, greenery drapes, garlands, bouquets)
- *Lighting elements* (spotlight, strobes, small white lights)
- *Historical elements* (period pieces, documents)
- *Signage* (banner, signposts)
- *Guests themselves* (period costumes, wearing fluorescent lights)
- *Accessories* (candles, balloons)

Depending on the size of the event, your own background, and how important each element of the decor is judged to be, you may have separate vendors for each element or you may do it all yourself.

If you are doing the decor yourself, remember to pay extra attention to the entrance and reception areas. These are the areas that make the first impression and where the majority of

Bright Idea

You can achieve a lot economically by clever use of lighted backdrops, especially behind buffet tables. Backdrops can be achieved by projecting enlarged photographs onto muslin screening. A good backdrop not only sets the theme for the event but also draws guests' eyes and decreases the need for props.

Simply Beautiful

Liese Gardner and Susan Terpening, authors of *The Art of Event Design* (Premedia Business Magazines & Media Inc.), provide the following decor tips:

- ○ To make a bold statement, consider a black-and-white color scheme, adding a fashionable accent color for flair.
- ○ Scale is very important. If possible, use huge decor elements at entranceways to create an impact and a sense of enormous space.
- ○ Skillful repetition is also key to successful design. But use your instincts, and avoid repeating your main elements too many times.
- ○ Streamline your event decor by looking at all elements of the design and taking away anything that's not absolutely necessary. Remember, less is more!

photographs will be taken. Also keep in mind that lighting is often a neglected decor element but is extremely important to mood and ambience. In fact, event planning veteran Martin Van Keken says, "It's the single most important element of an event." Lighting is also useful for creating special effects and for enhancing themes.

The goal of the event and the age of its attendees both help determine the use of space, in terms of decor and seating arrangements. For example, if the main purpose is to provide networking opportunities, then guests need to be able to move around freely, and the event site should be relatively free of chairs and other potential obstacles. On the other hand, if the attendees are all senior citizens, extra seating will be needed to ensure comfort.

3. *Catering*. Food and beverages have a well-established role in successful events. Earlier, we noted a trend involving increased attention to the nutritional value of foods. In addition, food presentation (i.e., the way food looks in a display or on a plate) is receiving a lot of attention. The French have said it for centuries: "C'est la presentation qui compte" (Presentation is what counts). The rest of us are only now catching on. If you are planning small events, you are less likely to encounter food sculptures or other more elaborate presentation effects, but

---

Smart Tip

Tip...

If you hire a decor expert, make sure to find out how much time is required for installation and to allow adequate access to the site. Goldblatt says, "I have seen decor budgets double when less than one hour was allotted for installation of a major set."

How Sweet It Is

Choosing menus can be a lot of fun. Just make sure you don't forget the dessert! Preferably a memorable one. (Fruit does not count. Sorry!) Barring a convention of diabetics, you or your client must come up with a dessert (or, even better, a choice of desserts) in your menu plans. This is true even if good nutrition is a major catering goal. Why? Because dessert is many people's favorite part of the meal. Not only that, its end position ensures leaving a lasting impression. Dessert is like a fireworks finale: It should outshine everything that precedes it.

The peril of omitting dessert is illustrated by one recent event. The dinner featured beautifully presented, delicious food, including a sumptuous fruit platter. Nevertheless, many disappointed murmurs ("No dessert . . . ?") floated in the evening air.

always make sure you hire a caterer who not only pays attention to the taste and nutritional content of food, but also provides a variety of food colors and textures.

If you discuss food choices with clients, you will undoubtedly consider customer preference and budget. Also keep in mind the following aspects of the event:

- *Formality.* Simpler foods work best with relaxed occasions. Reserve fancier food items for more formal events.
- *Theme or region.* If the event has a theme, match the food to it. When appropriate, consider regional cuisine.
- *Seating plan.* Foods requiring a knife and fork are best reserved for sit-down events. If guests will be standing, such as at a cocktail party, finger foods are preferable.
- *Overall "look" of serving stations or tables.* As noted above, food color is important to the presentation effect. A banquet choice of chicken, mashed potatoes, cauliflower, and white rolls suffers from several problems, among which is that all these items are white!

Encourage clients to choose foods with vivid colors like red, orange, and purple. (Yes, purple. And no, we are not suggesting dyed foods—purple cabbage makes a terrific garnish.)

Seating Chart

The following are the typical seating configurations for different event types:

- ○ *Banquet rounds.* This is the most frequently used seating for social functions involving food. Round tables are 60 or 72 inches in diameter and normally seat from eight to 12 people.
- ○ *Reception.* Smaller round tables with cocktail and food stations throughout a room.
- ○ *One long oval or rectangular table.* This type of table is ideal for small parties or meetings in which close interaction is desired.
- ○ *U-shape, T-shape, and E-shape, hollow square, and hollow circle styles.* These configurations are all created using 8-foot-long tables. These seating plans are ideal for committee or staff meetings.
- ○ *Classroom-, theater-, or auditorium-style.* Rows of chairs face the front of the room, either with or without desks. This seating style is used for corporate events involving presentations.

4. *Entertainment.* The possibilities for entertaining guests are virtually limitless. Keep in mind that usually the more involved the guests are, the better time they'll have. Just to get you started, here are a few ideas:

- *Performing arts* (dancers, musicians, singers, actors, comedians)
- *Mysticism* (fortune tellers, palm readers, magicians)
- *Circus* (clowns, acrobats, jugglers, tightrope walkers)
- *Carnival* (games, rides)
- *Kids' fun* (puppets, mimes, robots, ventriloquists, balloon artists)
- *Pastimes and sports* (croquet, horseshoes, miniature golf, volleyball)
- *Period performances* (jousting, chariot races, wandering minstrels)

Beware!

To keep your event both enjoyable and safe for all, consider following two recent trends:

1. Request that guests turn their cell phones to the vibrate option so that ringing phones don't disturb others, and

2. inform guests of all exits from the venue. In addition, make sure you have a written list of the venue's emergency procedures and that you have staff on hand who are trained in CPR and other emergency techniques.

Measuring Up

Use the following industry tips to help gauge serving requirements:

○ A gallon of liquid (punch, coffee, etc.) fills approximately 20 standard (8-oz) cups.

○ As a general rule, 30 percent of the coffee you provide should be decaffeinated and 70 percent regular, except in the evening, when the numbers are closer to 50 percent each.

○ Assuming a comfortable room temperature at the event venue, 65 percent of morning beverages should be hot and 35 percent cold. In the afternoon, beverages should be 35 percent hot and 65 percent cold. Guidelines are more difficult in the evening when the beverages offered depend greatly on the type of event.

○ Provide one server for every 20 to 25 people at a sit-down meal.

○ Provide one bartender for every 75 to 100 people, unless the event is primarily for cocktails. In that case, you may need one bartender for every 25 to 30 guests.

The Main Event— Putting It All Together

Once you have interviewed the client and done some preliminary brainstorming, you should have enough information to fill out the Event Design Worksheet," starting on page 36.

If you are just starting out in the event planning industry, make sure you have this worksheet or something similar filled out before you provide the client with a proposal containing an

Smart Tip

Include emergency phone numbers in your event records in case problems arise. Suppliers and any vendors not on-site for the event should give you numbers to call if, for example, any equipment malfunc-

event cost estimate (see Chapter 8). Note that your proposal need not detail every aspect of the event design.

Be aware that the production of a proposal is time-consuming and potentially expensive, especially if you include photographs or sketches. Sachs points out that only the larger companies producing high-end events can afford to provide clients with free proposals. You should receive a consultation fee (she suggests about $150), which can be applied toward a client's event if he or she hires you.

Maximizing the appeal of an event means making sure that all five senses are engaged. Engaged, but not overwhelmed. Goldblatt suggests providing not only sensory areas but also "neutral zones" whenever possible, especially if the event is a large one. Before finalizing the design, you should mentally "walk through" the event. What will guests see, hear, smell, taste, and touch?

Once you have a signed contract and a design that meets client approval, it is time to organize the details of the event.

Organization

During this decision-intensive phase, you will rent the site, hire vendors, and take care of even more details than you might believe possible. You'll be on the phone until your ear is numb. But before you do any of this, make sure you have a contact person (either the client or someone acting on the client's behalf) with whom you'll discuss all major decisions. Ideally, this person's name should appear on the client agreement (see Chapter 4). Having a designated individual helps ensure that communication lines are kept open. Also, social events in particular sometimes suffer from the "too many cooks" syndrome. Having one designated contact helps you avoid being caught in the middle of disagreements. "You don't want to find yourself caught between mother and daughter or husband and wife," says Sachs.

Generally speaking, the bigger the event, the more lead time required to plan it. Major conventions are planned years in advance. Although you may not be arranging

Event Design Worksheet

1. *Who?*
   Type of guest: _____
   Age group: _____
   Number of guests: _____
   Degree of guest participation: _____

2. *What?*
   Type of event: _____
   _____
   Style: _____
   _____
   Theme? _____
   _____

3. *When?*
   Date: _____
   Start time: _____
   End time: _____
   Invitations to be sent? _____

4. *Where?*
   Site (or site type): _____
   Guest lodging to be arranged? _____
   Transport to be arranged? _____
   Security services needed? _____
   Emergency personnel needed? _____

5. *Why?*
   Goal/purpose of the event: _____
   _____
   _____
   Publicity for the event? _____
   _____
   _____

Event Design Worksheet, continued

6. *How?*

   How should guests remember the event? (Prioritize the following.)

   ○ *Site*

   Type of facility: _____

   Location: _____

   Accommodations: _____

   Amenities: _____

   ○ *Decor*

   Major elements: _____

   _____

   Additional elements: _____

   _____

   ○ *Catering*

   Type of cuisine: _____

   Beverages/alcohol: _____

   Type of service (cocktail, buffet, seated table service): _____

   _____

   ○ *Entertainment*

   Music: _____

   _____

   Performance: _____

   _____

   Activities: _____

   _____

   Speaker: _____

   _____

7. *How Much?*

   What is the budget? _____

   Range of flexibility? _____

   _____

   _____

   _____

events on such a grand scale, you do need to allow at least a few months for events like corporate picnics, reunions, or large parties.

Begin by arranging for the following:

- *Site.* If applicable, you must have a signed contract for the site before any other plans can be made.
- *Air travel.* If your client's event requires it, air travel arrangements should be made as soon as possible after signing the site contract. With sufficient lead time, you can usually obtain group rates from most major airlines. Select a company that has experience with group travel and can advise you of the lowest fares available and the best routes for your attendees.
- *Ground transportation.* Depending on the event and the number of attendees, you may need to contract with a limousine service, a bus company, or a car rental agency to meet your needs. Normally, planners should arrange for attendee transportation to and from the airport, for guided tours, and to special events outside the site. Before you choose ground transportation services, compare the reservation, deposit, payment, and cancellation policies of several companies to make sure you get the best service.
- *Vendors.* Make sure you have done your homework and that you possess signed contracts.

Organization Checklist

Once these major decisions have been made, you will have many more details to deal with. On page 39, there's a checklist to help you, although you may not need to do all these things. Time frames are shown in a range to accommodate a variety of event sizes. Use this checklist and fill in any other tasks particular to your event.

Logistics

Effective organization requires logistical ability and knowledge of the following types of information, among others:

- *How many people you can comfortably get into a room.* This depends on the purpose of the event, the activities involved, and the space taken up by the decor.
- *Whether one buffet line will service 350 people.* It won't!
- *Where to put food service stations.* In areas with easy access for replenishing.
- *How long to allow for a cocktail reception.* Allow 30 minutes to an hour.
- *How to let guests know to begin eating.* An invocation or some other cue should do the trick.
- *How to be sure guests will have finished eating before the scheduled activities begin.* Build in a little extra time.

Organization Checklist

Stage I (30–90 days before the event)

- ❏ Reserve venue and accommodations
- ❏ Review budget (periodically)
- ❏ Contract with vendors
- ❏ Investigate licensing requirements
- ❏ Develop a marketing plan, if needed
- ❏ Make note of can't-miss dates in vendor contracts
- ❏ Invite speakers (after confirming availability)
- ❏ Schedule entertainment
- ❏ Send announcements or invitations to attendees
- ❏ Select audiovisual materials
- ❏ Contact suppliers of any items you handle yourself (e.g., rental items)

Stage II (15–60 days before the event)

- ❏ Send second announcements with information on hotel and travel arrangements
- ❏ Complete the activities list and the menus
- ❏ Verify arrangements with client, vendors, and suppliers
- ❏ Complete contingency/emergency plans
- ❏ Prepare evaluations
- ❏ Prepare list of temporary help needed

Stage III (10–30 days before the event)

- ❏ Finalize event setups, transportation, and guest accommodations
- ❏ Confirm reservation of audiovisual equipment
- ❏ Arrange for transport of audiovisual equipment to the site
- ❏ Submit a room list and pay a deposit to the site
- ❏ Complete airline reservations
- ❏ Hire temporary help
- ❏ Conduct orientation meeting/training of temporary help
- ❏ Send any event-related tickets to attendees

Stage IV (5–10 days before the event)

- ❏ Send all printed materials to the site (keep master copies for yourself in case materials are lost)
- ❏ Contact all vendors to confirm

Coordination

After you have made the initial plans, turn your attention to each of the activities that form a part of the overall event. At this point, your goal is to ensure that everyone is on the same wavelength. Good communication skills are important. Make sure all vendors have at least a general idea of the overall event schedule. Even more important, vendors should be clear about what is expected of them, and when. Vendor arrival times should appear in the contracts, but verify those times anyway. This is a "check and recheck" period. Make sure all your staff members know their roles. Remember, good communication is key. "Big projects can get out of control very quickly," cautions planner Joyce Barnes-Wolff.

Use a notebook (or your computer) to track the progress of each aspect of the event. While you will not record items that a vendor is responsible for providing (e.g., flowers ordered by the florist or food items the caterer orders), your tracking system should include all supplies and equipment your own business orders, as well as the names of suppliers, so you can verify them quickly. Use separate lists for items purchased and rented. On the following page is a sample of the information you might want to include in your records.

To maximize the effectiveness of your coordination efforts—not to mention minimize your headaches—remember:

- Delegate when possible.
- Anticipate change and be flexible.
- Have a backup plan for any critical aspects of the event.
- Share critical timing elements with vendors and site personnel.

Another way to minimize your headaches is to use a checklist like the one on page 41.

Evaluation

The obvious, and in one sense the most important, test of an event's success is customer satisfaction. The goal, of course, is to end up with a client who will sing your praises up and down the street, shouting it from rooftops. This is the client who will hire you again, perhaps for an even bigger (and more expensive) event. This is also the customer who will provide the famous word-of-mouth advertising for you.

Having a blissfully happy client does not mean you're home free, however. You can always improve, and additional evaluation will help you to do so. If you have employees, a round-table post-event discussion can bring to light aspects you may not have considered. Collect input from every team member. Your evaluation procedure should include an actualization, i.e., an accounting of your company's investment (hours

Sample Tracking Record—Items Rented

Item	Quantity	Use	Supplier	Date Received	Cost (Total)
linens-round	30	tables	AJ Linens	7/15/05	$174.80
linens-rect.	10	buffet tables	AJ Linens	7/15/05	$35.67
lanterns	25	lighting (grounds)	Lux Inc.	not received	$150.00

Coordination Checklist

Stage I (Day before the event)
- ❑ Review the program with site directors
- ❑ Troubleshoot with staff to overcome any problems
- ❑ Confirm arrival of all printed and audiovisual materials
- ❑ Confirm delivery of all rental items (or else pick them up)
- ❑ Tour the facility to confirm setups

Stage II (Day of the event)
- ❑ Check signage
- ❑ Verify that all rental items have arrived—tick them off
- ❑ Inspect all setups at least one hour before the event begins, checking off items in your notebook
- ❑ Test all microphones and audiovisual equipment
- ❑ Distribute evaluations at the event

Stage III (After the event)
- ❑ Return any kegs and recover deposits
- ❑ Distribute tips
- ❑ Write thank-you letters to client, site personnel, and vendors
- ❑ Review and approve all vendor bills for payment
- ❑ Have post-event evaluation meeting
- ❑ Compile all event data in one file and store in records

▲

worked, costs incurred) in the event. This procedure helps verify that you are charging clients enough to make a profit.

There are several other ways to evaluate the success of an event. One is to have a trained individual observe it and give you feedback. Such an individual could be an event planning consultant. Depending on the consultant's experience level and the type of event, you can expect to pay anywhere from $25 to $50 per hour, for 10 or more hours. A shorter session would probably mean a higher hourly rate.

This individual could also be a lay person, however. If you know someone who hosts extremely successful parties, consider asking that person to observe your event. Or get someone who plans fundraising events to help you in return for a generous donation.

Another way to evaluate an event is to get feedback from other industry professionals working at the event. The caterer and the bartender, among others, might be able to provide you with suggestions.

If the event is open to the general public (e.g., a community event), consider surveying the guests at the event. You can get immediate feedback this way, and most people you approach will cooperate. Talk to as many people as time allows, and take notes. Remember, the feedback you receive may not be very balanced. People may be swept up in the mood of the moment. Without time for them to step back and reflect, they may provide unwarrantedly positive or negative feedback. Conducting a mail or phone survey can eliminate this disadvantage, but you will not get the same level of cooperation. A response rate of 10 percent is considered average, so you will need to survey many more guests than you would with a face-to-face survey.

Sample Survey

Please rate the following aspects of this event by circling your response:

1. *Decor*	Excellent	Good	Average	Fair	Poor
2. *Food/beverage*	Excellent	Good	Average	Fair	Poor
3. *Entertainment*	Excellent	Good	Average	Fair	Poor
4. *Service*	Excellent	Good	Average	Fair	Poor
5. *Friendliness of personnel*	Excellent	Good	Average	Fair	Poor

We appreciate any comments you can provide us with:

_____

_____

_____

Thank you for your help!

However you conduct your survey, keep your questions to a minimum and keep them short. You can have people fill out the sample survey on page 42 at the event, or you could mail it to attendees.

Whatever combination of strategies you choose, Goldblatt advises, don't wait until the end of the event before collecting at least some feedback. Unless you know about them in time, it's impossible to correct details that might make the difference between an average event and a stand-out one. He also cautions that evaluation is another phase that receives too little attention.

Now that you know what is involved in each stage of the event planning process, we turn our attention to what you need to do to get your own business up and running. So grab a strong cup of coffee, or a large chocolate bar, or both. Then read on as we tackle the necessary paperwork.

In the
Beginning

This chapter details much of what you will need to do before you open your doors. We will cover naming your business, determining its structure, and finding a location. We will also take a brief pass at acquiring the necessary licenses, permits, and business insurance. (Well, you didn't expect every aspect to be fascinating, did you?) Finally, we will provide some sample documents you'll need to run your business.

What's in a Name?

Smart Tip

What have other event planners named their businesses? Check out the competition so that your name won't be too similar to theirs.

Quite a lot, as it happens. The right name can draw your target market to you. It can also single out your event planning business from others and keep it sharp in clients' memories. Before you decide on a name, consider what kind of planning you want to do, the scope you want your business to have, and whether you want to convey a particular image. Will you have a highly specialized service (e.g., only birthday parties) or an extremely general one (e.g., social and corporate events of all kinds)? Will your service be local, national, or international? Do you want to produce only high-budget events, or will you work in any price range? Depending on your answers to these questions, a good name for your business could consist of any of the following:

- *Description of your service* (e.g., Event Planning Inc.)
  Advantages: Helps potential clients hone in on you.
  Disadvantages: Creativity sometimes suffers.

- *The type of event you specialize in* (e.g., Birthday Bashes)
  Advantages: Helps clients find you. You'll get fewer calls for types of events that you don't plan.
  Disadvantages: Your specialization might change. What if you decide to do anniversary parties, too?

- *Your name* (e.g., Ann Smith Inc.)
  Advantages: People you meet while networking need remember only your name. If you use your full name, you may improve your personal credit rating as you build your business.
  Disadvantages: Customers won't know what type of business this is. Worse, the IRS could confuse you and your company. And if your company goes under, your personal credit rating may suffer.

- *Qualities your business embodies* (e.g., Elegant Evenings)
  Advantages: Helps establish the image you want to create.
  Disadvantages: Vagueness may make it tough for clients to find you. Also, this kind of name pigeonholes your business. You'll probably not be hired to produce a reunion or picnic.

- *Indications of the scope of your business* (e.g., Bloomington Event Planners Ltd.)
  Advantages: Anyone looking under city listings will find you.
  Disadvantages: Your scope might change. What if you want to branch out to other cities?

- *A combination of the above* (e.g., Benden's Classic Parties)
  Advantages and disadvantages: The whole is not necessarily the sum of the parts. Consider carefully the advantages and disadvantages of each part of a combination name to see which apply.

The outline above is not an exhaustive one, but it contains some of the best ideas for creating a name that will make your business a standout in event planning. Industry expert and consultant Patty Sachs cautions against limiting yourself by choosing too specific a name. Words like *perfect*, *elegant*, and *exquisite* lock you into formal or high-priced events, she says. Exciting words like fabulous, fantastic, and incredible are reserved for theme parties and entertaining events. On the other hand, if you're going to be highly specialized, she suggests names like Open House Planning, His 'N' Hers Parties, Wedding Weekends, and so on. Also, she cautions, "The word 'affair' has been done to death."

If you buy an existing business, you can take an element from the business's former name, or even use the whole name. New York City planner Jaclyn Bernstein, DMCP, kept half of the former name when she took over an event planning business. Thus her company's name had both a familiar ring for clients and enough of a difference to remind them that ownership had changed.

A good name is well worth the effort you'll put into finding it. With some thought, you can end up with a name as unique as your business.

Bright Idea

Look in the Yellow Pages, or wherever you plan to list your business, and find the category you'll have it listed under (e.g., Event Planning or Party Planning). Then choose a name that will put you at, or near, the top of the list. People looking for services often start at the top and work their way down.

The Name Game

After you've short-listed some ideas, ask yourself the following questions about each name:

- *Is it easy to pronounce?* People are reluctant to say a name they're unsure of. This reluctance could be fatal in an industry that relies heavily on word-of-mouth advertising.

- *Is it short enough?* Length affects ease of pronunciation. Plus, you and your employees will have to say this name all day on the phone and still have time to do other tasks. Thus Supercallifragilistickexpial delicious Inc. is probably not the best choice, even if you specialize in children's events. (This name suffers from other problems, too, but we won't go into those.)

- *Is it easy and logical to spell?* If somebody hears your company name but can't find it in the phone book because of a spelling problem, you will lose potential clients.

- *Is it memorable?* If possible, avoid a name that sounds too ordinary.

▲

Places, Everyone!

The type of events you'll plan and the size of your business are among the factors that will determine where you set up shop. Event planning businesses can be run from home, in retail or commercial space, or from a vehicle.

If you're starting small, a homebased event planning business may be the ideal choice for you. This option keeps overhead low and saves travel time to and from the office. One potential problem is that friends and family might drop in at all hours because you're "not really working." Be firm. Set up business hours and stick to them.

You may find that you need more space than your home office can provide. In this case, retail or commercial space can be the perfect setup for you, especially if you expect to have some foot traffic or if you specialize in a particular type of event. Deborah Williams and Kim Quigley, who plan both corporate and social events, decided to locate their business in the now-trendy Deep Ellum, a historical, artsy area of Dallas. Jaclyn Bernstein maintains her business in a fast-paced business district in midtown Manhattan. This location is important for her company because she focuses on corporate events.

The disadvantage of renting space is primarily the cost. Rent, utilities, phone lines, and parking are all considerable expenses. Downtown locations are especially costly.

Executive suites also make sense for event planning businesses. They provide you with a good business address, a professional atmosphere, phones, and other business equipment. Sometimes executive suites will even provide a shared secretary.

If you go to clients rather than having them come to you, a car or van might work as your headquarters. Keep in mind, however, that if you need a computer for your business, you'll have to either invest in a laptop or keep part of your office elsewhere.

Wherever you locate, make sure that your business does not violate zoning ordinances, rental agreements, and the community welfare. This holds true for all kinds of event planners.

Consider stockpiling space if you expect to grow quickly or store a lot of equipment so you won't have to move.

> ## Tip...
>
> ## Smart Tip
> Whatever your location, consider the following points:
> - ❍ Planners of local parties do well in central locations.
> - ❍ Convention planners should locate near the major convention sites and hotels in their cities; similarly, a meeting planner should be situated in a central business district.
> - ❍ If you plan nonlocal events, your proximity to an airport may be paramount.

Brand-New Baby

You have to do more legal stuff for your newborn business than new parents have to worry about. On the other hand, you'll probably be way ahead in the sleep department, which means you'll have some working brain cells available for the tasks that lie ahead of you.

In Fine Form

No, this is not "101 Ways to Shape Up Your Body While You Shape Up Your Business." We're talking about the legal form your business will take. Small businesses usually operate as one of the following: sole proprietorship, general partnership, limited partnership, corporation, or limited liability company. All these forms are thoroughly discussed in Chapter 2, "Business Structure," in *Start-Up Basics*. The majority of event planning businesses are either sole proprietorships or corporations, so we'll do a quick review of them here.

A sole proprietorship is the easiest (and least expensive) form in which to start a business, because you need no paperwork, unless you're using a name other than your own (see the bullet point on "Fictitious name license" on page 50). There are no separate tax forms either, and taxes are lower than they are for other business forms. But consider the meaning of *sole*. You are the only owner. If your business fails, your personal credit rating may be ruined. If you're starting small, however, the risks are usually minimal. Indeed, as long as you are operating small, David Granger feels it's a great way to run a business.

Industry expert Patty Sachs operated her own business in Minneapolis as a sole proprietorship for many years and never had a problem with this legal form.

Joyce Barnes-Wolff, who runs her own event planning business in Ohio, also has a sole proprietorship. "It's easy and quick," she says. "For me, this works the best." However, most banks are not eager to lend money to sole proprietorships, she points out.

A corporate structure is often advantageous to a business because the corporation exists as a separate entity. It alone is legally responsible for its actions and debts. As an employee of the corporation, your personal assets are protected in most situations, even though you may own all or most of the stock. Deborah Williams and Kim Quigley turned their partnership into a C corporation on the advice of their attorney. "You could lose your home, your car, everything, with a partnership," says Deborah.

> **Bright Idea**
> Consider sharing space with a related business. For example, you could set up shop with a party supply store or a caterer. You might not only save money but also gain referrals. If you elect to share space, however, make sure you have a clear contract stating how space and responsibilities will be shared.

According to industry expert John Daly, the decision to incorporate depends partly on how much you have at stake. In his opinion, small events are not usually a problem, but once you're doing huge ceiling treatments, you don't want to risk wiping out your personal assets. The main points to remember? Incorporation protects you. However, increased paperwork and taxes are disadvantages.

If deciding on a legal form for your business keeps you up at night, consider two things: First, your nails will grow back. Second, as the above examples illustrate, your business structure is not carved in stone. It can be changed.

The Words and the Fees—Licenses and Permits

Most cities and counties require business operators to obtain various licenses and permits to comply with local regulations. For everyday operation of an event planning business, you may need the following:

- *Business license:* ensures proper zoning and parking
- *Fictitious name license:* allows you to do business under a name other than your own
- *Vendor's permit* (varies from state to state): allows you to buy and resell

---

The Right Idea

Any original idea in a unique form can be protected under U.S. copyright. This includes cartoon characters, sculptures, paintings, plays, maps, songs, scripts, photos, books, and poems, to name but a few. There are five classes of copyrights:

1. Class TX: Nondramatic literary works (fiction, nonfiction, advertising copy, textbooks, etc.)
2. Class PA: Works of the performing arts (drama, music, choreography, etc.)
3. Class SR: Sound recordings (independent of musical or literary works)
4. Class VA: Works of the visual arts (pictures, graphics, models, maps, ads, etc.)
5. Class RE: Renewal registration (works originally copyrighted before January 1, 1978—all classes)

Why, you may ask, do you need to know about this? If you come up with an original logo for your service or for a type of event that you produce, you might want to copyright that logo. Similarly, you might write a script for a particular type of original event (e.g., a murder mystery/dessert party) and want to copyright it.

To apply for a copyright, send a copy of the work with an official form and a $30 application fee to the Copyright Office, Library of Congress, 101 Independence Ave. SE, Washington, DC 20559, (202) 707-3000. For more information, consult its Web site at www.copyright.gov.

- *Health department permit:* if you also cater events and thus handle food
- *Liquor, wine, and beer licenses:* if you yourself serve alcohol
- *Sign permit:* covers size, location, and sometimes the type of sign you may use
- *County permits:* may be applicable if you are located outside city limits

Depending on the event, you may also need the following:

- *Fire Marshall permit:* for large gatherings, events with fireworks, or the display of a vehicle indoors
- *Special event permit:* if you'll be using city property
- *Street closure permit:* for closing off a street (e.g., a block party or arts festival)
- *Parade permit:* self-explanatory!

Check local regulations to see which of the above licenses and permits you'll need. But no matter where your event will take place, you may need to apply for the following types of permission:

- *Copyright permission.* The two major U.S. music-licensing companies, Broadcast Music International (BMI) and the American Society of Composers, Authors, and

---

Making Your Mark

Atrademark is any name, word or symbol with which a business identifies its products, services, or organization. Legal protection for trademarks depends on how distinctive the law considers the trademark in question. Generally, names that are not in common usage (e.g., arbitrary, fanciful, or coined terms) receive protection.

Why should you care? If, for example, you invent a product like the murder mystery/dessert party we mentioned in "The Right Idea" and name it Peaches and Scream, you might want to trademark the name of the event.

Because you cannot register a mark with the Patent and Trademark Office (PTO) before you use it in conjunction with some product or service, you must protect your mark during the development stage by keeping it secret (this is known as a trade secret). Once you use your trademark properly on your product—by adding superscript "TM" or "(T)"—register it with the PTO. For more information about trademarks, consult the following publications produced by the Patent and Trademark Office:

○ *Basic Facts about Registering a Trademark*

○ *Official Gazette—Trademarks*

If your library does not have these publications, you can order them from the U.S. Government Printing Office by calling (202) 512-1800. You can access its Web site at http://bookstore.gpo.gov.

Publishers (ASCAP), recently decided to enforce their rights to collect fees. You may need copyright permission to use text materials, music, audiovisual displays, photographs, drawings, ads, drama pieces, or any number of a variety of materials. Always check for the copyright of any materials you use in an event. We do not suggest this lightly or out of a desire to "cover our act," as it were. The fact is, many artists and companies take copyright infringement very seriously. Therefore, so should you.

Smart Tip

Some cities provide packets with explanations and all the forms you'll need for the various licenses and permits, so investigate this possibility. Also, it's a good idea to ask more than one city or county employee about the licenses you need, especially if you get information that is confusing or not what you expected.

- *Trademark permission.* Be aware that distinctive trademarks are protected. Trademarks apply to products. For example, you may need permission to use any relevant brand names on literature you circulate about an event or about your business.

Even if your event planning business does not need a particular type of permit, always make sure that your vendors are properly licensed and have the appropriate permits.

Damage Control

Knowing what kind of insurance to carry and how much to obtain is an important aspect of good risk management. Chapter 7, "Business Insurance," in *Start-Up Basics* provides detailed information on all types of insurance. As the owner of an event planning business, you are most likely to need the following types of insurance:

Beware!

If you operate your event planning business from your home, you may need additional coverage. Your homeowner's policy may be sufficient, but if you plan to store or use expensive machinery, such as a computer, or if customers or clients will visit your home for business purposes, you may want to purchase additional coverage.

- *General liability insurance.* This is the one type of insurance you must carry, and every business owner interviewed for this book had it. Many event sites will be unavailable to you if you don't carry this coverage. General liability insurance protects a business against accidents and injuries that might occur at the event site or at your office. You may be liable for bodily injuries to customers, guests, delivery people, and other outsiders—even in cases in which you have exercised "reasonable care." As David Granger points out, "If I put down lighting and someone trips over a cord that wasn't taped down, or if one of my centerpieces catches fire, or if a stage prop falls, I need to be covered." It's a good idea to carry 1 million dollars worth of liability insurance. In fact, Dallas planner Deborah Williams says local hotels won't do business with event planners who don't carry at least 1 million dollars in liability insurance.

- *Workers' compensation insurance.* If you have employees, you may also want this type of insurance. Williams has it for employees at Designs Behind the Scenes. You are liable for injury to employees at work caused by problems with equipment or working conditions. In every state, an employer must insure against potential workers' comp claims. However, employee coverage and the extent of the employer's liability vary among states.

- *Auto insurance.* Cars and trucks are sources of liability. Even if you own none, you can be liable for injuries and property damage caused by employees operating their own or someone else's car while on company business.

Smart Tip

Whenever possible, consider replacement-cost insurance, which will replace your property at current prices, regardless of the cost when you bought the items. (Computers are an exception to this rule. Because the technology changes so quickly, the equipment can become obsolete and therefore almost worthless.) Replacement insurance offers protection from inflation. But make sure that your total replacements do not exceed the policy cap.

- *Bonding.* If you sell large numbers of airline or entertainment tickets or any of several other types of goods, you may need to carry bonding. This procedure requires you to put aside money into a separate account for reimbursing clients for tickets they purchased from you in the event your business goes under. You may also need bonding to protect you if one of your employees steals or damages something at an event site. Vendors should carry their own protection. Check your state's legal requirements.

Hashing It Out—Proposals and Agreements

To do business (and protect your company as you do it), you'll need a variety of documents. Invoices and purchasing orders for an event planning business are, for the most part, the same as those for any other business. So we will concentrate our attention on proposals and several different kinds of agreements.

Proposals

Quite simply, proposals tell clients what you will do for them and at what cost. A proposal hits the high points of your creative idea(s) for the event. It is an important selling tool and might consist of any or all of the following elements:

- *History of your company.* Provide one if relevant.

- *Letters of reference.* Kudos from clients for whom you planned similar events work wonders.

- *Write-ups.* Often a complimentary newspaper or magazine article featuring your business is a valuable tool for selling your services to others. You may also want to include photographs.

- *Description of the event.* This is where you sell your ideas. Walk the client through the event, describing what guests see, hear, smell, taste, and touch. What emotions will guests feel?

- *Description of services.* This tells which vendors you'll hire and sketches out how you'll achieve what you write about in the description of the event.

> **Smart Tip** Tip...
>
> Remember, your proposal is a selling tool. If your description of the event bores you, it will probably bore the client, too. Use active verbs and vivid adjectives. Also remember that you want to "sell" the prospective client on your ideas before cost is mentioned. Therefore, make sure the event cost estimate appears at the end of the proposal.

- *Listing of additional services.* If you also will provide catering, floral design, or some other service, describe those services completely.

- *Production schedule.* This item lets the client know any pertinent details about the timing of the event, especially if there are critical aspects to arrange. If you're hosting a smaller event, you usually do not need this part of the proposal.

- *Event cost estimate.* This accompanies any proposal (see Chapter 8 for details).

Customers must be able to visualize the event when they read your proposal. As David Granger puts it: "Proposals need to be flowery." His colleague, Deborah Williams, agrees: "Dave is phenomenal at proposals," she adds. "When you read one of his proposals, you can just see the whole thing."

You have to figure out a way to make clients visualize the event as you have designed it, and they have to understand the quality of your work. Consider including in your proposal some photos of a previous event you planned that was similar to what the client wants. Any photos included should, of course, be vivid and lively. Jaclyn Bernstein stresses the importance of asking clients a lot of questions and listening well. Catching (and using in your proposal) exact words customers have used in discussion with you helps to convey a sense of excitement about the event, she says. Enthusiasm is important, as long as your language isn't too extreme.

Agreements

The possession of signed documents detailing all aspects of the events you produce is not only helpful but also imperative to the legal health of your business.

> **! Beware!**
>
> Make sure you include in your proposal an expiration date for the event cost estimate. You don't want to be expected to produce that event for the listed price five years from now!

Following is a description of the different types of event planning agreements.

- *Client agreements.* Once the client has agreed to hire your company, you need an official contract. The exact form this contract appears in will vary by state because you must conform to state code. If you draft your own client agreement, get a local attorney to take a look at it.

    We provide a sample agreement, starting on page 56, to give you an idea of elements you may want to include in your own agreement.

- *Vendor agreements.* Any vendor providing a service for your client's event should sign a formal agreement with your planning company. As with any legal document, get your local attorney's advice. Starting on page 58 is a sample agreement with a catering company.

- *Site agreements.* Once you have selected the site that will best suit your client's needs, confirm your arrangements with the site's sales representative and ask for a written contract or letter of agreement. Review the contract carefully and clarify any misunderstandings or ambiguities with the site representative. The contract should include the arrangements for guest rooms and any activities scheduled to take place at the site. Contracts should also include the site's cancellation and deposit policies.

Any site contract with a hotel or other lodging facility should state that if fewer rooms are occupied than expected, you will not be held responsible. Instead, attendees should be given a deadline before which they can claim a room in the reserved block at the group rate. After the deadline, any unreserved rooms are made available to the general public.

With luck, you now have a good idea of how to name your business, decide on its legal form, and find a location. You also know how to acquire the necessary licenses, permits, and insurance and how to draft agreements. (See, that wasn't so bad, was it?)

In Chapter 5, we'll tackle a subject that's always interesting: money. To be more precise, how to get it and how to spend it.

Beware!

Make sure that any vendors you hire are properly insured and/or bonded. They must carry insurance to protect their companies (and you) from their negligence, bankruptcy, or lack of appearance at an event. Any forms of insurance or bonding that they carry should be listed in the vendor agreement (see page 58).

Smart Tip

Tip...

Be sure to make allowance in your proposal cost estimate for unexpected on-site expenses, such as audiovisual equipment or last-minute printing.

Sample Client Agreement

This agreement is between Right Touch Event Planning Inc. (hereafter referred to as PLANNER) and Mr. John Doe (hereafter referred to as CLIENT).

I. *PLANNER agrees to provide:*
- ○ Research, design, organization, coordination, and evaluation of the CLIENT's Silver Wedding Anniversary
- ○ A social event to begin at 8:00 P.M. on Saturday, May 23, 2004, at the CLIENT's residence and to end by 2:00 A.M. the following day
- ○ Comprehensive general liability insurance to cover damage caused by any action, or inaction, of the PLANNER or of any individuals contracted by the PLANNER
- ○ Vendors as agreed upon with the CLIENT (see attachment)
- ○ Additional staffing for the event

II. *CLIENT agrees to provide:*
- ○ The CLIENT's residence as site for the event
- ○ The CLIENT's kitchen and equipment therein for use by the caterers and bar staff
- ○ One individual to serve as decision maker for the PLANNER
- ○ Decisions in a timely manner
- ○ Homeowners' insurance to cover damage caused by an act of God or by any action, or inaction, of the CLIENT or of the CLIENT's guests

III. *FEES*

The PLANNER will receive a commission amounting to 15 percent of the total event cost. The total event cost is not to exceed $10,000.

IV. *TERMS*

The CLIENT agrees to provide payment for the services described. This payment shall be remitted to the PLANNER according to the following schedule:

Upon signing of this document:
- ○ 50 percent of total event cost, based on estimate
- ○ 25 percent of commission, based on estimated event cost

May 24, 200x:
- ○ Remainder of final event cost
- ○ Remainder of commission, based on final event cost

V.   *CANCELLATION*

Should the PLANNER cancel his or her services for any reason other than acts of God, the CLIENT shall receive a refund of all pre-paid fees, less any expenses incurred on behalf of the event. Should the CLIENT cancel the event, the following payments shall be due:

○ Cancellation more than 60 days before event: 25 percent of estimated event cost and 50 percent of commission

○ Cancellation between 15 and 60 days (incl.) before event: 75 percent of estimated event cost and 50 percent of commission

○ Cancellation less than 15 days before event: 100 percent of estimated event cost and 75 percent of commission

VI. *FORCE MAJEURE*

This agreement is automatically canceled if the event is interrupted by an act of God, by war, or by strikes.

VII. *HOLD HARMLESS and INDEMNIFICATION*

The PLANNER and CLIENT agree to hold one another harmless from negligence and to mutually indemnify.

VIII. *ACCEPTANCE OF FULL AGREEMENT*

This agreement, plus attachments, constitutes the full agreement. Any changes to this agreement must be approved in writing by both PLANNER and CLIENT. Those parties affixing signatures below agree to accept the terms and conditions of this agreement.

_____   _____
Client   *Date*

_____   _____
Planner   *Date*

Sample Vendor Agreement

This agreement is between Right Touch Event Planning Inc. (hereafter referred to as PLANNER) and Sweetness and Light Catering Inc. (hereafter referred to as VENDOR).

EVENT DATE: May 23, 2004
EVENT ARRIVAL TIME: 7:00 P.M.
EVENT START TIME: 8:00 P.M.
EVENT STOP TIME: 2:00 A.M. May 24

I. *VENDOR agrees to provide:*
   ○ Ten trays of hors d'oeuvres, as detailed in attachment
   ○ Buffet dinner for 40 persons, as detailed in attachment
   ○ Dessert buffet, as detailed in attachment
   ○ All serving equipment, including, but not limited to: trays, tongs, chafing dishes, and buffet ranges
   ○ Serving staff, as detailed in attachment
   ○ Cleanup crew, as detailed in attachment
   ○ Proof of insurance

II. *PLANNER agrees to provide:*
   ○ Complimentary parking for VENDOR and staff
   ○ Utilities (gas, electricity, water)
   ○ Kitchen facilities
   ○ Tables and table linens
   ○ One individual on-site to act as liaison with vendor
   ○ Liability insurance for the event

III. *FEES*
   PLANNER shall provide the following payment to VENDOR:

Hor d'oeuvres	$300
Buffet dinner (40 persons)	$600
Dessert buffet	$450
Serving and cleanup	$180
Subtotal:	$1530
Less referral fee	−$80
Total:	*$1,450*

Sample Vendor Agreement, continued

IV. *TERMS*

PLANNER shall pay VENDOR a deposit of 50 percent ($725) upon execution of agreement. Balance due by June 23, 2004.

V. *CANCELLATION*

If the VENDOR cancels for any reason, he or she shall forfeit all funds received or due and shall repay PLANNER any funds advanced for this event. If the PLANNER cancels for any reason, he or she must provide the following payments to VENDOR:

- ○ Cancellation more than 60 days before event: Refund of referral fee ($80)
- ○ Cancellation between 15 and 60 days (incl.) before event: 25 percent of total fee
- ○ Cancellation less than 15 days before event: 75 percent of total fee

VI. *FORCE MAJEURE*

This agreement is automatically canceled if the event is interrupted by an act of God, by war or by strikes.

VII. *HOLD HARMLESS and INDEMNIFICATION*

The PLANNER and CLIENT agree to hold one another harmless from negligence and to mutually indemnify.

VIII. *ACCEPTANCE OF FULL AGREEMENT*

This agreement, plus attachments, constitutes the full agreement. Any changes to this agreement must be approved in writing by both PLANNER and CLIENT. Those parties affixing signatures below agree to accept the terms and conditions of this agreement.

_____   _____
Client   *Date*

_____   _____
Planner   *Date*

5

No Guts, No Glory—
Acquiring and Spending Money

As most people discover early in life, acquiring money is a lot harder than spending it. To start your event planning business, however, you will have to do both of these things. In this chapter, we will focus on financing your business and buying equipment.

On Target

The start-up, or pre-opening, period is a trying time, in more ways than one. First, it demands much of you—in patience, determination, and resources. A great deal of time and energy, not to mention money, must be invested to get your company on its feet and running smoothly. Second, the start-up period will find you trying out numerous ideas and discarding some of them. Of course, this book, combined with the other research you will do, should help minimize your mistakes. Still, the pre-opening period is a time for learning and should be treated as such. Benefit from your early experiences so you will operate more efficiently and not repeat mistakes once the business has become established.

Totaling Up

Before you do anything else, estimate your business expenditures over the start-up period and over the first six months of operation (see Business Expenses Worksheet on page 63). If you have filled out the "My Own" column in the Start-Up Expenses Worksheet on page 21 in Chapter 2, put those figures in the "Start-Up" column. If you have not yet made those estimates, now is the time to do so.

First, work horizontally. Add the "Start-Up" figures and the "First Six Months" figures to produce the "Total Cost" figures for each row. Then, working vertically, add up the "Total Cost" figures. The "Total Required" figure is the approximate amount you will need to start the business and keep it running for six months.

Note that this business expense work sheet includes no costs for planning particular events. You will incur these costs even if you plan no events at all. In that sense, then, these are all fixed costs. When you contract to plan an event, you should receive a deposit from each client to cover some of the immediate costs associated with producing that event (e.g., vendor deposits). The price you charge a client for planning an event will cover not only your costs for that event but also some fraction of your fixed costs.

> **Beware!**
> Do not underestimate your communications budget. If you have multiple phone lines, a cellular phone, a pager, Internet access, etc., these are ongoing expenses. Joyce Barnes-Wolf estimates her monthly communications costs to be her second largest expense, after labor.

In Chapter 8, which deals with financial management, we'll discuss how to price your planning services and how to figure out a break-even point for your business. For now, you need an approximate idea of how much money you'll require for your business and your own living expenses until your company makes a profit.

How long will this be? As with many aspects of this industry, it depends. New York City planner Jaclyn Bernstein bought an existing business, and her company was profitable within six months. Event planner Joyce Barnes-Wolff made a small profit in her business's first year. It was enough to pay herself a salary but not enough to reinvest in the company.

As we've mentioned, event planning businesses can often take two or three years to break even. Therefore do not assume that you'll make a profit within six months. Play it safe, and plan for a longest-case scenario. Include a reasonable living allowance for yourself into your calculations. This allowance will vary greatly, of course, depending on your own circumstances and your local cost of living.

Once you have an idea of your capital requirements, it is time to think about your financing options.

Going for the Green

To find your best source of financing, look in the mirror. Most entrepreneurs invest their own resources first, and so should you. Your own capital is immediately available, carries no interest obligation, and requires no surrender of business equity. Event planner Martin Van Keken used money from the sale of another business. Nearly all entrepreneurs we interviewed used at least some of their own

> **Bright Idea**
>
> Don't forget other financing sources besides savings. Sometimes certificates of deposit (CDs) and other investments can be cashed in to provide funds. For example, as her start-up capital investment, Joyce Barnes-Wolff used part of her retirement fund from a previous position.

Business Expenses Worksheet

	Start-Up	First Six Months	Total Cost
Rent/deposit			
Equipment			
Inventory			
Licenses and taxes			
Phone/utilities			
Payroll			
Advertising/promotion			
Legal fees and accounting			
Vehicle maintenance/mileage			
Misc. (postage, signage, office supplies, etc.)			
Total required			

money. With regard to financing, an event planning business is no different from other companies. Chapter 4, "Getting Financing," in *Start-Up Basics* covers financing in detail, so we'll keep our discussion brief.

Getting any venture off the ground can be a very costly proposition—one that may be beyond your immediate cash reserves. If this is the case, the following are other avenues you can explore to obtain the necessary capital:

- Friends and relatives
- Banks
- The Small Business Administration (SBA)
- Credit cards
- Equity
- Venture capital

Besides self-financing, the most frequent sources of financing for the event planners we interviewed were friends, relatives, and banks. For example, to help Williams and Quigley start Designs Behind the Scenes in Dallas, the latter's father co-signed their bank note.

If there is any single piece of advice most appropriate for the new entrepreneur in need of money, it is to make a careful assessment of the proposed value of the business, the amount of capital needed to finance it, in what increments it is needed, and the period of time you'll need the capital for. You'll need a business plan. You have made one, right? If not, go back to Chapter 2. (Do not pass GO. Do not collect $200. However, a good plan will help you collect a great deal more than that.)

Once you have your start-up money, it's time to go shopping.

The Right Stuff

You'll need some equipment and inventory for your company. In this section we'll discuss the must-haves and the nice-to-haves for event planners.

Before you go out and spend thousands of dollars, make a list, check it twice, and trim it well. Industry expert and author Patty Sachs advises new owners of event planning businesses to keep start-up costs low by buying only the minimum equipment and supplies. You need basic equipment, letterhead, business cards, a computer bookkeeping program,

Profile

Dallas planner Deborah K. Williams knows how to bargain. She found stellar deals on both rent and insurance rates. By renting in a then-unfashionable location and taking excellent care of the property, she gained a loyal landlord who locked in her rent at a low rate. Similarly, by giving all her insurance business to a small company, she saved a bundle. "I wheeled and dealed," she says.

license or permit fees, Internet service, and brochures or fliers to get you started. You will also need insurance, but you should not need inventory (e.g., party supplies). Says Kim Quigley, "We bought on an as-used basis."

Equipment

Most event planners use standard office equipment such as copiers, fax machines, and computers. Many planners use meeting management software designed specifically for their field.

Small event planning businesses may not require much equipment. But no matter what the size of your business, invest in the following must-haves:

- *Vehicle.* You can use your own car, but you will need a vehicle for visiting clients and traveling to and from event sites. Using your own car will reduce the amount of start-up capital you need. Other options are to lease or purchase a company vehicle.
- *Office furniture.* Good quality used furniture may be an option. You'll need a desk, chair, filing cabinets, and bookshelves.
- *Cellular phone or pager.* Several planners said they feel cellular phones are an indispensable part of doing business in the event planning industry. Some entrepreneurs use their pager and cell phone together to save money.

Cruising the Net

As you undoubtedly know, you can access many different types of resources online. These include local, national, and global news; entertainment; professional and financial data; and reference materials such as those provided in a well-stocked college library. You can use online services and the Internet for research, whether it is for your own business or for a client, and you can network with vendors and other planners. Helpful Web sites abound (see the Appendix). Online services are also good for making contact with consultants and other individuals who can offer valuable advice. You can even conduct business online with clients in other parts of the world if necessary. This is one aspect of the information highway that can be especially beneficial for homebased entrepreneurs.

If for no other reason than having the possibility of reaching valuable information sources, planners who subscribe to one or more online services or the Internet have a distinct advantage over those who do not.

- *Multiple phone lines.* One phone line is usually not enough. Install a multiline (push-button) phone system, allowing you to switch back and forth between lines while on one phone. In general, you'll need one phone line for every five employees (if you have any, that is).

- *Answering machine or voice mail.* You must provide a way for clients, vendors, and others to leave messages in your absence.

- *Computer.* A computer is essential not only for producing professional-looking proposals, but also for keeping records and tracking information. It is a valuable time-saver to be able to pull up a proposal for a previous event, make the necessary adjustments and then send the proposal to the new client. A computer is also necessary for using the Internet, a valuable tool for event planners.

> **Profile**
>
> Designs Behind the Scenes' business card and letterhead features a rendering of the Dallas skyline. Kim Quigley says that from the get-go, the creation of a striking image was a priority well worth the investment. "Your business card should be impressive," she says. "We get compliments constantly."

You do not necessarily need a high-end computer. One possible strategy for deciding what kind of computer capability to invest in is first to decide what software you'd like to use and then pick a computer with enough memory to run that software. Chapter 8, "Computers," in *Start-Up Basics* discusses computer purchases in detail.

- *E-mail and Internet access.* If your business has a national scope, and you plan events in distant locations, you can save yourself a lot of time and money by going online to find hotels, caterers, and other services for your event. Even if your business is on a smaller scale, e-mail makes communication easy and convenient, and the Internet can help you find potential new customers. It can also help you research a variety of topics and find suppliers. In addition, all planners we spoke to have Web sites to give potential customers information about their companies and the work they do. Whether you use a modem, cable, or other means of accessing the Internet, make sure you still have a phone line available for receiving calls.

- *Printer.* The ability to send out professional-looking proposals is important, and you'll need a printer to do that. Unless your business does very high-end events, however, a good inkjet printer should be fine. Make sure you pick one that is compatible with your computer.

- *Digital camera.* The ability to show clients your work online can be valuable. However, a traditional camera might be sufficient if you have a good scanner. Digital cameras carry a wide price range, from $150 to $550.

- *Software.* Virus-detection software is a necessity, and you must update it regularly. You might want to invest in one of the office suite software packages, discussed in

Chapter 8, "Computers," in *Start-Up Basics*. Consider also software designed specifically for event planning. (See the Appendix for more information on how to contact the vendors of all the programs described here.)

There are five main types of software you may need: a word-processing program, a spreadsheet program, a relational database, desktop publishing software, and specialty software.

There are many software programs available now. We provide only a few examples here. For more information about software, consult the Web sites provided in our Appendix.

1. *Word processing program.* Allows you to write text. Used for writing evaluations, forms, letters, lists, and anything else you want to write. Most planners we spoke to use Microsoft Word. Make sure you have a recent version (approximately $80).

2. *Spreadsheet program.* Helps you manipulate numbers. Used for producing outlines, schedules, timelines, budgets, and calendars, among other uses. Excel (about $100) is often cited by event planners, as is Quicken. The latter costs anywhere from $30, for the most basic version, to $90 for a more luxurious version.

3. *Relational database.* Allows you to manage, update, and use information from other databases. Used to produce name badges, receipts, reports, tickets, etc. If you are planning only small events, you may not need this type of software.

    Meeting management software packages often include several different types of software, including programs that let you handle attendee registration, track sponsored events, generate reports on various records and expenses, generate confirmation letters, and print name badges for attendees. One meeting management software package is MeetingTrak, supplied by Gomembers (cost: $3,000). Certain Software Inc. has introduced Meeting Planner Plus ($2,000, but enrollment in their free two-week demonstration will halve the cost). This package is designed to offer planners an all-in-one solution to managing the many details involved in producing an event. It features multiple databases and side-by-side display of vendor quotes. It also provides customizable reports, lists, and timetables, among other features. Complete Event Manager (approximately $400), from EKEBA International, also handles many aspects of event management.

4. *Desktop publishing.* Gives your products a polished look. Used for name badges,

---

Tip...

Smart Tip

Create a database of all your vendor information, including products/services, prices, policies, and delivery times. By having this information computerized and retrievable within seconds, you will drastically reduce your time and work. Just make sure you also have a Rolodex or some other hard copy of the list, in event of a computer failure.

posters, press releases, signage, tickets, etc. Microsoft provides both Microsoft Publisher ($130) and Microsoft Publisher Deluxe ($150).

5. *Specialty software.* Allows you to perform specific tasks. Used for name badges, place cards, signage, tickets, diagrams, floor plans, etc. For example, room design software lets you design floor plans for meetings. Once you enter the room's dimensions, you can place elements such as walls, doors, and seats in various arrangements until you reach the best one for your event. Room Viewer, by TimeSaver Software, is one such program (approximate cost: $500). Another specialty software program lets you design and produce name tags. PC/Nametag Pro II ($300) is a product of PC/Nametag.

There are many other items you might need. If you have a larger business, some of the following equipment items may be necessities. For smaller companies, these may fall into the nice-to-have category.

- *Walkie-talkies.* Jaclyn Bernstein and her employees often use walkie-talkies to communicate on the job. You can buy a basic walkie-talkie for $40; a high-end one will cost $150.

- *Laminating machine.* Bernstein also has a laminating machine to make signage for the events her business produces. Cost of this equipment ranges from $50 to $250.

- *Typewriter:* Handy for filling out forms, a typewriter may also help you out of a temporary computer emergency.

- *Copier.* If your company makes more than a few hundred copies per month or if you don't have time to keep running out for copies, you should consider investing in a copier to save time spent going to the copy shop. For $300 to $500, you can buy a multifunction machine that combines the functions of printer/copier/fax machine.

- *Scanner.* This piece of equipment is occasionally handy to have, but it's not essential for event planners. If you don't already have one, you're probably better

---

Smart Tip

Tip...

If you want high-quality name tags but won't need many, you don't need to buy the software. PC/Nametag will sell name tags to you already assembled at reasonable rates ($1.25 to $4.50 each, depending on your order size). Contact them at (800) 233-9767 or at www.pcnametag.com.

Profile

Jaclyn Bernstein frequently gives thank-you gifts to clients. These range from the relatively small (e.g., a New York cheesecake, a T-shirt, or cookies in the form of New York taxi cabs) to the more costly (e.g., a crystal apple). All are designed to remind the client of her mid-town Manhattan business. Showing appreciation and making the client feel special are important parts of doing business, she says.

off buying a digital camera so you can avoid scanning your photos into your Web site. If you do buy a scanner, you'll note a large quality/price range. The simplest scanner costs about $50, and the most deluxe one, capable of scanning not only documents and large stacks of photos but also slides and negatives, is about $300.

- *Fax machine.* Most entrepreneurs benefit from being able to fax documents to clients. You may be able to fax from your computer.

Keeping It All Together—Inventory

Some planners store an inventory of decorations and props. However, most rent these as needed, especially large items like gazebos and arches. You must consider both the storage space requirements and the maintenance requirements of inventory, as both will affect your overhead costs. Remember, unless you store only very small, low-maintenance items, you'll need more space and employee (or your own) time devoted to inventory upkeep. And no matter what kind of inventory you stock, you'll have to spend time tracking it.

How many smaller inventory items (e.g., centerpiece items, candles, etc.) should you stock? That depends in large part on whether you handle event decor yourself or contract it out to a designer or decorator. Most of the event planners we talked to hire

---

Finders Keeper

If you have at least a small amount of space for inventory, you may find it worthwhile to buy a bargain item when you see it, rather than on an as-needed basis (especially because you'll never find it when you need it!). If you stick to items that have fairly general uses (e.g., centerpieces), you decrease the chances of having your purchases merely gather dust on your shelves.

In their book, *The Art of Event Design* (Primedia Business Magazines & Media Inc.), authors Liese Gardner and Susan Terpening suggest the following sources of decor bargains:

- ○ Thrift stores
- ○ Garage and yard sales
- ○ Antique stores
- ○ Flea markets
- ○ Home and garden shops
- ○ Farmers' markets
- ○ Ethnic markets

---

vendors to provide decor. Therefore, they stock very little inventory. And so should you, at least at the beginning. As a rule, you should buy items as you need them. Most planners we talked to had no start-up inventory costs at all.

So what do planners routinely keep as inventory? Those we interviewed listed the following items:

- *Photos and videos.* Most planners keep photos of events their companies have produced. This industry is a very visual one. "People want to see what you've done," says David Granger. Many planners put photos on their Web sites as well as use them in portfolios and keep them in resource cabinets.

Beware!

Don't forget less obvious costs. These can include, but are not restricted to, items such as the following: association memberships, subscriptions to industry publications, small promotional gifts, a new-business open house, custom colors for special print pieces, professional portfolio creation, van rental for transporting larger equipment, and T-shirts or uniforms for your hired helpers for larger events.

Start-Up Checklist

Equipment

❑ Vehicle
❑ Office furniture
❑ Phone
❑ Phone line(s)
❑ Answering machine or voice mail
❑ Cellular phone/pager
❑ Computer
❑ Printer
❑ Scanner
❑ Digital camera
❑ Software (general)
❑ Software (event planning)
❑ E-mail/Internet access
❑ Web site

❑ Fax machine
❑ Copier
❑ Typewriter
❑ Laminating machine
❑ Walkie-talkies

Inventory/Miscellaneous

❑ Vendor catalogs
❑ Client gifts
❑ Fabric
❑ Floral containers
❑ Lighting
❑ Misc. (office supplies)
❑ Misc. (write in)

- *Vendor catalogs and brochures.* Joyce Barnes-Wolff has several resource cabinets filled with these. Well-chosen catalogs and brochures are a good source of ideas and valuable reference aids for unusual items.

- *Gifts.* Several planners stock gifts for clients. Jaclyn Bernstein keeps a variety. Martin Van Keken stocks gifts of silver-plated yo-yos with the company logo.

- *Fabric.* Fabric accounts for most of Martin Van Keken's inventory. He has an extensive collection, upon which he relies heavily. David Granger keeps three-ring binders of linen swatches. Some planners, like Jaclyn Bernstein, own table linens.

- *Floral containers.* Most planners keep containers for floral arrangements. These include urns, wrought-iron stands, and bowls for floating arrangements, besides the more traditional vases. Williams, Quigley, and Granger rent plants and other items as part of their business. Their table-top décor ranges from statuary items to antique hat boxes. If you use a florist or greenhouse, however, your floral-container needs will be minimal.

- *Lighting.* Most planners either rent lights or hire a lighting company. And they buy candles for specific events.

Our suggestion about equipment also holds true for inventory: Buy only what you need to get started. Most items should be acquired on a per-event basis. To make sure you are ready to start up, fill in the checklist on page 70.

Once you have bought the required equipment, inventory, and other supplies for your event planning business, it's time to consider hiring the help you'll need.

With a Little Help from My Friends

Every planner needs assistance of some kind in putting together a special event. In this chapter we will provide suggestions for the kind of help you'll need and how to find it.

▲

Hiring Personnel

Event planners have two types of personnel: permanent staff and temporary help. The percentage your company has of each of these types will depend on the size of your business, what you can afford, and your own preference.

The planners we interviewed had between two and 12 permanent employees. Deborah Williams and Kim Quigley did not hire any permanent employees for the first three years. Their company now has 11, counting themselves. Joyce Barnes-Wolff, however, prefers a smaller company, with only herself and an assistant as permanent employees.

All planners hire temporary personnel, often in large numbers, on an as-needed basis. For example, Vancouver planner Martin Van Keken, whose company has 12 permanent employees, hires anywhere from 10 to 150 temporary employees, depending on the size and complexity of the event. In areas with well-defined on- and off-seasons, business owners staff up during busy times. Part-time employees may help set up and tear down an event site. They might also be servers or ushers. Part-time workers are ideal for office tasks such as entering data into the computer and addressing and mailing envelopes.

Someone, whether yourself, a permanent staff member, or a temporary employee, will be needed to fill each of the following roles:

- *Office manager:* oversees and coordinates employees and may also handle administrative, clerical, and office-supply duties
- *Planner:* helps plan events
- *Sales staff:* sells events to clients; networks to gain additional business
- *Designer:* handles decor if you do not hire vendors to do that
- *Public relations representative:* handles public relations involving clients, vendors, suppliers, and the general public
- *Director of marketing:* takes charge of advertising and promotion; often, the public relations representative and the director of marketing are the same person
- *Bookkeeper:* tracks all business and per-event expenses, and may also prepare tax returns; if you hire an accountant to do these tasks, you may not need a bookkeeper
- *On-site assistant:* helps set up and tear down at the event site

> **Tip...**
>
> ## Smart Tip
> Besides according their employees flexibility, another way event planners keep their workers happy is to give them the space to do their jobs. People don't like to feel others "breathing down their necks." Remember, you had enough confidence in your employees to hire them in the first place. So let that confidence show.

- *Setup staff:* greets guests, helps run registration or concession stands, serves food and/or drinks
- *Craft services staff:* provides help with craft items, preparation of invitations, etc.
- *Kitchen staff:* cleans up
- *Gofer:* runs errands
- *Driver:* delivers supplies to the venue

Note that the above list is about roles, not titles. There is considerable variety in titles given to employees, but whether you use informal titles or more formal ones (e.g., production coordinator, account manager, operations assistant), the tasks are the same.

Bright Idea

Stop periodically and write out two lists: a "Priorities in my business life" list and an "Actual time spent" list. Compare the lists. Are you spending the greater proportion of your working life on the activities to which you give a high ranking? If not, maybe it's time to reorganize.

Each employee should have a job description that outlines the objectives of the job, the responsibilities of the position, the working conditions, and the relationships of the position to other jobs. Owners and employees should all have a clear idea of where everyone fits into the company. Columbus, Ohio, planner Joyce Barnes-Wolff also stressed the importance of staff members understanding and supplying input for each other's projects.

The smaller your business, the more different tasks any one staff member will perform. There is no ideal number of employees, but however many you hire, obey what is a golden rule in this industry: Keep good employees happy. As New York City planner Jaclyn Bernstein puts it, "You have to be friends when you work crazy hours with these people."

Working together in the event planning industry, often at "crazy hours" and under deadline pressure, demands teamwork to an unusual degree. As with any cooperative effort, a willingness to compromise and to be flexible is essential for both employers and employees. Most planners we interviewed spoke of teamwork. All who had staff, whether permanent or temporary, were glowing in their praise of them. "They're the best," says industry expert and business owner John Daly. "They're amazing. I couldn't do a thing without them."

"We make a good team," says Dallas planner Deborah Williams.

Smart Tip

Don't forget to write your own job description, advises industry expert John Daly. It's important to stay focused on what your goals are, too. Knowing which responsibilities you want to handle will make it easier to decide which tasks can be delegated to others.

Just Rewards: Salaries, Wages, and Benefits

What kind of salaries do planners give their staff? That depends on the area of the country as well as on the employee's experience level and amount of responsibility. An inexperienced worker with only moderate responsibilities makes anywhere from $18,000 to $32,000. An experienced employee with heavy responsibility probably makes between $25,000 and $45,000.

If you hire temporary help in coordinating an event, industry expert Patty Sachs says, the average wage is $10 to $15 per hour for setup staff. Craft services staff make $7 to $10 per hour.

You can pay other temporary or part-time employees either hourly or per event. They usually earn $6 to $9 per hour. If you decide to pay your intern (which will make attracting one easier), consider an hourly wage somewhere between minimum wage and $8 per hour or offering a stipend, i.e., a flat amount compensating the intern for a specific amount of time, usually for the duration of the semester. Stipends can range from $350 to $800 per semester. If your intern is a graduate student trained in some facet of event planning, you should expect to pay anywhere from $10 to $14 per hour, depending on responsibilities and the area of the country.

Knowing that their employees often go above and beyond the call of duty during crunch periods, several event planners mentioned flexibility in employees' work times. Other common employee benefits include trips to professional conferences in desirable locations, generous amounts of time off and company-funded professional training. Employers typically also offer group health insurance to full-time staff. They may also provide life insurance and retirement plans.

Joyce Barnes-Wolff joined the local chamber of commerce to provide benefits for her employees. "I needed insurance I could not afford on an individual basis," she says. "It's more affordable as a member." Keep in mind that full-time employees will cost you between 15 percent and 30 percent above their wages or salaries, depending on the benefits you offer.

Team Picks

Chapter 6, "Employees, Benefits, and Policies," in *Start-Up Basics* offers thorough advice on hiring personnel, but those in the event planning industry also have advice to give about choosing staff members. "The single most important thing to succeed," stresses Martin Van

---

Bright Idea

If a local college offers courses in event management or related areas (e.g., travel and tourism, hotel management), part-time employees and interns should be easy to find. Contact the head of the department and ask about the internship program. Local chapters of industry associations such as ISES and MPI may also offer internship referrals. And you can look on the Web (see the Appendix).

Keken, "is to create a very, very reliable team around you."

"Don't be afraid to hire really good people," advises Daly. "Hire somebody as good as you or better."

Joyce Barnes-Wolff cautions that you shouldn't hire people too similar to yourself. If you surround yourself with employees who think the same way you do, she says, you won't have help in your weak areas. Look for skilled employees with professional strengths and personality traits you don't have.

Bright Idea

Remember, you are working in a "fun" industry that often involves celebration. Consider a weekly, or monthly, office celebration. Bring in something simple, like cookies or doughnuts. Anything of this nature improves office morale. If you want a good motto to do business by, consider one of author and industry consultant Patty Sachs': "Don't Wait—Celebrate!"

Choosing Vendors

As a planner, you must find and retain a team of professionals to provide the specialty products and services required to put together an event. Depending on the type of event, you probably need to hire one or more of the following vendors:

- *Art director:* handles design, computer imaging, etc.
- *Caterer/bartender:* serves food and beverages
- *Calligrapher:* handles lettering on invitations and signage
- *Decorator:* provides decor
- *Florist:* provides floral arrangements
- *Graphic artist:* designs and executes event posters or invitations
- *Photographer/videographer:* photographs, records, and preserves the event
- *Performer:* provides entertainment
- *Transportation/parking personnel:* drives and parks vehicles

Playing It Safe

All the planners interviewed for this book agree that finding the right vendors is a crucial aspect of creating a successful event. Remember, even if a mistake is a vendor's fault, the mishap will reflect on you because you are managing the event. That's what makes researching vendors so important. David Granger picks his with extreme care. "Choosing vendors means knowing them and trusting them," he says. As do most event planners, Jaclyn Bernstein makes her choices with long-term relationships in mind. She has even had business come her way through vendors who know her.

Joyce Barnes-Wolff has "the best Rolodex in the Midwest," she says. So she knows who's right for an event. "I can pull in the best people from across the area."

Martin Van Keken places extreme importance on vendor selection. "They're part of our team," he says.

As you research vendors, record the following information:

- Vendor name, address, contact information
- Area of service
- Prices
- Lead times required
- Payment policy
- Refund policy
- Discounts offered
- Specialty items/services

Beware!

Before you hire any vendors, make sure they carry the proper insurance (see Chapter 4) and meet any other legal requirements. A valet-parking service, for instance, needs to be insured, and perhaps bonded, in case a valet damages a car while he or she parks it. A caterer needs a food-handling permit and insurance. Even entertainers may need to carry insurance.

Inside Out

In their book, *The Art of Event Design* (Primedia Business Magazines & Media Inc.), authors Liese Gardner and Susan Terpening point out several benefits of working with individuals from outside the special events industry. Not only is this a good way to add style and distinction to the events you plan, such a strategy can also be a money-saver. Consider the following possibilities:

- ○ *Art students.* You can end up with interesting and inexpensive centerpieces if you get art students to make them for you. Check out the art department at the nearest college or university. Also take a look at the theater department if you need costumes or a backdrop for an event. Sometimes rentals are possible.
- ○ *Art dealers.* See if you can rent paintings for an event.
- ○ *Music students.* Need a pianist for an event? Consider the nearest school of music. Many students studying for master's degrees or doctorates will perform for a fraction of the cost of hiring a professional.
- ○ *Window dressers.* Go window-shopping and find out who designed the displays you admire. That individual may make an excellent decor consultant for you.

These are only a few of many possibilities. Use your imagination! But because these individuals may not have their own insurance, make sure you have coverage for anyone on-site during the event.

This vendor file is extremely important because it can save you hours of research time down the road, Sachs says. By having all this information right at your fingertips, you'll be able to conduct your vendor searches more effectively. Keep building this file as each new event comes along. A computerized file can be even more of a time saver.

Before you hire a vendor for the first time, find out all you can about the company's history. Ask for letters of reference, too. Once you are satisfied, make sure you have a document indicating what the company will do for your event. Vendor proposals should include the following elements:

Beware!
Food and beverages, and the servers that go along with them, are an important part of most special events. In fact, the catering bill often accounts for 40 percent of an event's budget. So pay special attention to choosing the caterer. Ask what the company's specialties are. Also ask to sample every item from the event menu before signing the contract.

- Complete description of service
- Description of equipment vendor will provide
- Listing of additional services vendor will provide, if any
- Description of costs and payment terms
- Scheduling information
- Proof of insurance, bonding, and other risk-management practices
- List of vendor requirements (water, electricity, etc.)

In addition, make sure these details all appear in the vendor agreement (see Chapter 4 on page 58).

Consulting Professionals

Every event planner we spoke to uses professionals for consultation. Some consultants you will pay directly, while others receive their payment indirectly.

The Direct Approach

The professionals most consistently hired in this industry are accountants and attorneys. But you may need the services of any one of the following professionals:

- *Accountant.* A good accountant will be your single most important outside advisor and will have the greatest impact on the success or failure of your event planning business. You will have to decide if your volume warrants a full-time bookkeeper, an outside accounting service, or merely a year-end accounting and tax-preparation service. Even the smallest unincorporated event planning businesses employ outside public accountants to prepare their financial statements. All planners interviewed for this book told us they have an accountant.

- *Attorney.* Finding the right lawyer early is critical. Make sure you hire an attorney you can trust and be comfortable with. You may need your lawyer to help ensure that your business is in compliance with licensing and insurance regulations. A lawyer can also check documents before you sign them and help you draft documents like vendor and client agreements. And, of course, an attorney will help resolve any legal problems that may arise. However, do not wait until you have legal difficulties before hiring a lawyer.

- *Business consultant.* You may consider hiring a professional to analyze your business plan and check your ideas for feasibility. A good consultant can keep you from making costly mistakes.

> **Tip...**
>
> ## Smart Tip
>
> Some venues have exclusive contracts with vendors or have a list of preferred vendors. If the venue does not, then decide on the caterer first and ask for referrals to other vendors. Often arrangements run smoother if the vendors frequently work together. Make sure the contract clearly states what permits and other contractors (e.g., waste removal firm) the catering company will be responsible for.

Coming to Terms

There are some points on which you can negotiate when hiring vendors, especially as your experience and reputation grow. As a general rule, the more often you have worked with vendors, the more leeway you can reasonably expect them to accord you. Consider asking about the following:

- O *Payment terms.* Get your required deposit as low as possible. Also, ask about a prepayment (i.e., paying in full before the event) discount.
- O *Complimentary sample* (e.g., food-tasting). This point is especially important either when hiring a vendor unknown to you or when you are asking for something outside the vendor's normal style of service.
- O *Complimentary extra.* When you provide a lot of business for vendors, they may be persuaded to throw in something at no charge. For example, a florist who provides centerpieces and other floral arrangements for a large event may provide a free bouquet for the guest of honor.

- *Event planning consultant.* This individual can help you with all stages of planning an event. If you are new to the industry, consider hiring a seasoned planner whose niche does not overlap with yours.

The Indirect Approach

Do not overlook the importance of individuals whose services you do not pay for directly. These individuals include the following:

- *Banker.* The right banker can be a tremendous asset to an event planner. Sometimes, in spite of contracts, clients (especially large corporations) do not pay their deposits on time, says Jaclyn Bernstein. Event planners, however, have to pay vendor deposits. This problem can create a financial crunch for you. However, a banker who has a good, long-standing relationship with your company may "float" you the required funds. "You need a good banker in this business," she says.

- *Insurance broker.* Another professional you do not directly hire is your insurance broker. Get one who will work with you. If you buy several types of insurance from the same company, you should receive a more attractive deal on the package. Deborah Williams gave all her business to a small insurance company and saved well over 50 percent on her liability insurance.

Off and Running

Remember, investigate well and give careful thought to hiring those who will work with you. The time you invest in choosing your employees and other professionals will pay off in the end as you create a solid, smoothly running team for your business.

Once you have your team, it's time to get the word out! Chapter 7 focuses on how to advertise and market your services and how to improve your customer service.

Profile

Martin Van Keken's company is self-financed, but he still relies on good banking relationships. And he doesn't hesitate to demand good service. "If I don't get what I need, I'll take my business elsewhere," he says. He also points out that even if you are asking for a loan, you should expect and receive good service. "You should be treated as a proper client. You should never, ever, be afraid to stand up for what you feel is right and to negotiate with your banker."

Profile

Jaclyn Bernstein and her partner, Robert Hulsmeyer, believe strongly in loyalty toward employees. Their New York City company, Empire Force Events Inc., lost nearly $2 million worth of business in the wake of the 9-11 tragedy. But unlike many New York companies, Empire Force Events did not respond with massive staffing cuts. "We did not lay any of our staff off," says Jaclyn.

You Can Always Get What You Want—
Attracting and Keeping Clients

If this proverb depresses you, don't worry. Once you have read this chapter, you'll know not only how to build a good client base but also how to keep it built up. You'll learn strategies for getting the word out about your business and for developing superior customer service. We'll also cover ways to capture the goodwill of your community.

Developing a strong client base can be one of the trickiest aspects of running an event planning service. Most planners' clients come by word-of-mouth, and while standard methods of advertising such as direct mail and magazine ads are often used to attract potential customers, nothing can compare to a referral from a previous client.

For your business to thrive, you will need to combine a variety of advertising strategies until you acquire a "Best in the Business" reputation. Chapter 10, "Advertising and Marketing," in *Start-Up Basics* covers these topics in detail. In this chapter we'll provide suggestions to guide you though the process of developing your strategy and help you evaluate the advertising media commonly used in the event planning industry. We'll also look at several other ways you can promote yourself and your new business.

Madison Avenue

Some new event planners spend hundreds of dollars on big ads in business magazines or in the Yellow Pages and wait for the calls to roll in. Dr. Joe Goldblatt, CSEP, founding director of the Event Management Program at George Washington University in Washington, DC, says this is a mistake: "When was the last time you spent $10,000 on someone in the Yellow Pages?"

Goldblatt advises new entrepreneurs in this industry to "stay away from the mass market." While a listing in the Yellow Pages may help potential clients find you, spending large amounts of precious advertising dollars targeting the general public is usually not effective.

Dallas planner David Granger agrees. The problem, he notes, is that customers need to see what you do, and a word ad won't accomplish that. He recommends networking and making friends in the industry. That way, he says, "People know you, trust you. They want honesty and integrity."

Industry expert and veteran planner John Daly doesn't use traditional advertising. He networks. He's active in industry organizations like NACE (National Association of Catering Executives) and ISES (International Special Events Society.)

Networking can help your business in two ways. If people have met you and know what services you offer, they may refer business to you or use your service themselves.

Bright Idea

Consider sending out mailings in the form of invitations, inviting the potential client to a wonderful theme party (or whatever your specialty). Provide a description that paints a vivid picture of the event. Remember the image you want to project. If you plan parties, the "look" of the invitation should be happy and fun, perhaps using neon colors. Use your imagination!

Furthermore, networking with hotels, caterers, and so on will give you a chance to meet some of the people whose services you may need as you plan events.

Although networking and word-of-mouth are the most common industry strategies for acquiring clients, traditional forms of advertising do have their uses. A distinctive card or brochure sent to a mailing list or to local businesses may attract new clients. A small ad in a local business magazine can help build name recognition. A Web site on the Internet may allow you to attract customers unresponsive to other forms of media. We will briefly discuss all of these below. Keep in mind, however, that potential clients will want to know what you've planned before, and they may require references.

Mailing It Out

Direct mail is one strategy to consider, as long as your mailing list is well-chosen. David Granger says that while word-of-mouth is their most effective advertising, Designs Behind the Scenes uses mailing lists of the organizations they belong to (ISES, MPI, NACE, and the Dallas Convention and Visitors Bureau).

Going Glossy

Regional magazines can be useful if you plan both corporate and social occasions. Because the market area for this kind of event planner can extend throughout a given county, a magazine focusing on that county can be an excellent one in which to advertise. These magazines can be geared to topics related to your service (e.g., gourmet food, floral design) or aimed at readers in a certain region. An ad in a regional magazine might be a good tool for reaching upscale consumers. A regional business magazine ad would reach prospective corporate clients.

Directing Traffic

Some event planners (although none we interviewed) advertise their services in the local commercial telephone directory. If you decide to go this route, be careful to do the following:

- *Choose the most appropriate category.* If, for example, you do primarily parties, you may want to be listed under Party Planning rather than Event Planning. It may even be worthwhile to advertise in more than one category by cross-referencing your listing.

- *Meet the directory deadlines for advertisements.* Missing deadlines can mean going a whole year without advertising.

- *Make your ad stand out.* Very few advertisers in the Yellow Pages and other directories make an effort to create hard-working, distinctive, benefit-oriented ads. They don't identify specific product or service benefits or include compelling ad copy, and most descriptions are virtually identical to those in neighboring ads. Don't make these mistakes.

Tip...

Smart Tip

Maximize your chances of success by making sure your company brochure (or any other information you provide) matches the type of business you have. All materials should look professional, but unless you have a high-end event planning company, a too-glamorous brochure can send the wrong message—and send potential budget-conscious clients running in the opposite direction.

Web-Weaving

The Internet is one of the best ways to reach a national, even global, audience. According to Nua.com, a compiler of Internet statistics, almost 10 percent of the world's population now has access to the Internet, and there are more than 581 million Internet users worldwide. Nua.com forecasts that the number of worldwide Internet users will reach 1 billion by 2005.

There are several advantages to marketing your service on the Internet, especially the World Wide Web. Because it's still largely unregulated, the Internet is an equal playing field for all. You can easily compete with larger competitors—even look like one yourself—without spending a fortune. By creating and maintaining a Web site in-house or seeking out a good, low-cost Web designer, even the smallest homebased business can afford a professional-looking, high-quality Web site. Many of the planners we interviewed use their Web sites to reach national and international client bases. Says event planner Jaclyn Bernstein, "Web sites are great for showing what your company does." However, she cautions that Web sites can't show everything, and that few clients will hire a planner based solely on a Web site.

Beware!

A brief word on ethics: Remember, save your promotion efforts for the right place and time. During an event is not the right time. As Vancouver planner Martin Van Keken points out, this is the client's event. "I have no right or authority to start promoting myself," he says. By the same token, do not allow your vendors to promote their companies at an event.

Be Creative!

As stated at the beginning of this chapter, strategies like networking and garnering word-of-mouth referrals are how most event planners acquire new clients. The importance of referrals presents a Catch-22 for new entrepreneurs: How do you go about building a client base when you have no previous clientele or vendors to rely on?

If you don't already have useful community contacts or previous experience within the event planning industry, you'll have to get creative. Industry consultant and author Patty Sachs suggests some ways to get your name out there:

- *Pass out business cards to everyone who comes into contact with you.* This includes vendors, suppliers, those who serve you (your hairdresser, etc.), and other business owners.

- *Offer a free resource search service.* This is a good way to win friends and stock your information file at the same time.

- *Give "introductory offer" discounts.* Many people are more willing to try a new service if they can do so economically.

- *Donate a certificate, redeemable for several hours of your planning services, to fundraising events in exchange for printed promotional consideration.* This strategy enables you to both advertise and gain a client who might later refer others to you.

- *Volunteer your help in planning a charity event.* A well-chosen event can provide you with a lot of exposure as well as community goodwill.

- *Keep an eye out for new businesses, and make yourself known to them.* Even aside from the clients you might gain, being friendly is seldom a waste of time.

- *Send a press release, complete with your photo, to the local paper.* Helpful hint: Black-and-white photos reproduce better in newspapers.

- *Plan your own open house.* Don't forget press releases and invitations to the press.

- *Create an event with another related business, preferably one that's established.* This idea may be less expensive than listed above.

- *Join a networking group and meet other businesspeople.* Widening your circle of business acquaintances is always a good idea.

> ## Profile
>
> New York City planner Jaclyn Bernstein has effective strategies for gaining clients. Early in her company's history, she produced an event for one company at cost, figuring that the company would return. She was right. Sometimes she'll even throw in a complimentary "extra" if she feels it will improve an event. "That company will come back with an event for twice as many people, with twice the budget," she says.

- *Join an online chat group of event planners* (see the Appendix). You can gain friends and ideas this way.
- *Collect the names of good vendors and encourage them to pass along your business card by offering them a commission on any jobs that they send to you.* Make sure that you reciprocate.
- *Send good photos of events you attend to the event hosts, together with your business information.* If possible, include a brief, personalized note mentioning how much you enjoyed the event; properly handled, this can be a good method of getting your name out to those who might use your services in the future.

Profile

Event planner Martin Van Keken of MVKA Productions in Vancouver feels strongly about the importance of service. When a client wonders if something is feasible, his company thoroughly investigates it. His team is always looking for the new and the different. "Just going out of our way isn't good enough," he says.

This One's a Keeper

How do you keep clients coming back? By paying close attention to three crucial (and interwoven) aspects of your business: customer service, public relations, and company image.

Serving It Up

Any business owner—or customer, for that matter—knows the one essential ingredient in running a successful business: customer service. You can be hard-working and dedicated, construct a flawless business plan, and have a bottomless source of financing, but if you don't keep customers satisfied and coming back, your event planning business will never succeed.

One of the best ways to keep customers coming back is to be constantly on the lookout for new ideas and for ways to improve the service you provide. Toward that goal, consider the following:

- *Take a course* (or even a series of courses) in event management
- *Invest in an hour* (or more) with an industry consultant
- *Attend other events* to study how they are produced
- *Attend as many arts-related functions* as possible (e.g., arts exhibits, theatrical performances) to gather ideas
- *Join trade organizations* (see a "Organization's the Key" on page 90)
- *Subscribe to at least one* professional newsletter or journal

Goodwill Hunting

Besides providing excellent customer service, earning (and keeping) the goodwill of clients and the community is important. Volunteering your company's help in planning charitable events will win you many friends in the community. And you are sure to gain loyal clients if you are willing to do the following:

- *"Go to the wall" for clients.* All the event planners we interviewed mentioned the need to "make it right," at all costs. This could involve anything from a planner's ability to handle last-minute emergencies to a willingness to "throw in" something extra for free, simply because the planner feels the event would be incomplete without it.

- *Offer clients something they can't get elsewhere.* Many planners mentioned the original aspect of the work they do. More and more, clients want the "different" and "unusual."

At Your Service

If you choose to volunteer your planning services, industry consultant Patty Sachs has some advice for you. First, be sure that the events are ones in which you want to specialize. If you want to focus on board meetings, don't volunteer to plan a birthday party—time spent researching balloon types is not going to help you. Also be sure that the events are high-profile, such as a charity ball or a meeting for members of your city's chamber of commerce. These are the types of events that will be attended by people who may become potential clients. Finally, Sachs says, make sure to get credit for your work—have the phrase "Event Planned by Jane Doe, Anytown, State" delicately yet prominently added to all fliers, invitations, and signs promoting the party, as well as all programs or other materials handed out at the event. If a press release regarding the event is mailed to the local newspaper, be sure you and your company are mentioned somewhere in the release. If the client doesn't intend to send out a press release, consider doing so yourself.

Keep in mind that although volunteering involves a lot of work for no obvious monetary gain, the payoff can be big in the long run. The contacts you make through these first few events will expand into a solid base of satisfied clients who can recommend an experienced, proven event planner to their friends, family, and business associates. Remember, many event planners give their initial clients big discounts in the beginning anyway, because they know it's unfair to charge full price for their inexperience.

- *Make clients feel valued.* Many planners mentioned gifts that they give to clients. These can include everything from cookies and other edibles to unusual decorative items to elaborate floral arrangements. Besides giving gifts, however, there are other ways to make sure clients know they are appreciated. A simple note with a personal message to convey thanks, congratulations, or birthday wishes can mean a lot, as can a phone call. Some planners also entertain clients for lunch or dinner.

- *Think less in terms of services and more in terms of problem solving.* Says Joyce Barnes-Wolf, "We try to listen to clients' needs and facilitate them within their budget. When you have budget restrictions, it forces you to become creative."

Beware!

Make sure that every document that leaves your office, whether it's a proposal, a brochure, or a simple business letter, is grammatically correct and well-written. Nothing creates a worse impression more quickly than grammar and punctuation errors and misspellings. Yet few things are easier to fix! If English was not a strong school subject for you, get a friend, family member, or employee to help. *And take the time to proofread.*

Organization's the Key

There are several large organizations that serve the special events industry. Most entrepreneurs we interviewed belong to ISES (International Special Events Society), NACE (National Association of Catering Executives) and MPI (Meeting Professionals International). Most also belong to their local convention and visitors bureau. Some belong to the Better Business Bureau as well.

The annual Special Event is the largest and highest profile industry trade show. It is put on every January by Primedia Business Magazines & Media Inc, publishers of Special Events Magazine. This trade show attracts a couple of thousand attendees from around the world.

If you are planning small-scale events with a local focus, you can still benefit from attending the national (and international) conferences. In addition, investigate local and regional organizations in your area. Involvement in industry organizations can provide you with ideas, valuable learning experiences, and excellent ways to network and become known in the event planning industry.

You're Only as Good as Your Last Event

Image—the way your company and its services are viewed by the public—is very important. Some event planners, therefore, will direct much of their advertising and promotion dollars toward building a good company image. You will have to decide how much you can afford to spend to establish, improve, and maintain your image. Increased revenues may be able to compensate for this expenditure.

Most important by far, however, is what your events say about your business. As the above very common industry saying implies, the quality of the events you produce is the most powerful shaper of your company's image and reputation.

Don't forget that small details also reflect on you and your company. Remember, Goldblatt cautions, "From the selection of vendors to the choice of brochure paper, every decision you make reflects your taste and company image."

Spot Reduction

Good customer service includes the ability to create memorable events while working within clients' budgets. Note, however, that this does not mean compromising your reputation to cut costs. While you and your client must both be reasonable about what can be achieved with a given budget, consultants Goldblatt and Sachs have provided some suggestions for keeping costs down. Your clients (or perhaps you yourself) can save money in the following areas:

○ *Catering*. Choose buffets over banquet service. This will reduce the serving staff required. Also, instead of providing a variety of alcoholic beverages, consider serving a signature drink (an original drink created for the occasion) to all guests.

○ *Decor*. Balloons are a good choice for decor. They are colorful, festive and inexpensive. Also consider having guests dress in costume or providing inexpensive decorations for guests to wear (e.g., glow-in-the-dark necklaces or bracelets, Hawaiian leis). Concentrate decor efforts on the entrance or reception areas because these are the areas that create first impressions and that are most often photographed. Finally, you might be able to share decor with another event being held within a few days of yours.

○ *Scheduling*. If an event can be shifted to an off-peak season, this strategy might result in some savings. Remember, the equipment-rental business is often seasonal. Although labor costs are usually not negotiable, renting in the off season can save money. Remember, too, vendors also often have a slow season.

▲

As we have previously mentioned, it takes most event planning entrepreneurs two to three years to turn a healthy profit. Use your start-up period to solidify business contacts, expand your industry knowledge, and develop a reputation you can be proud of. If you do this, profit will follow. To make sure you hang onto your profits, check out the financial management suggestions in the following chapter.

8

Right on
the Money

In this chapter, you'll find the basic dos and don'ts for managing your business's money. We'll suggest ways to maintain good cash flow. You'll learn how to arrive at an accurate pricing of your services and how to figure the break-even point for your event planning business. We'll also provide a few tax tips.

▲

Financially Speaking

How you manage your financial assets may determine whether your business succeeds or fails. Your capital is not merely a collection of money and property, but a powerful business tool deserving your careful attention. Because going into business for yourself is such a risky proposition, this capital should yield a higher rate of return than an ordinary investment would. Making capital work for you requires careful management of your business, especially of your current and future assets.

Financial management is an area many small-business owners neglect. They get so caught up in the day-to-day running of their businesses that they fail to take a good look at where their money goes. Most leave the responsibility of managing their finances to their accountants, who diligently prepare the proper financial statements at least once a year. (To learn how to generate financial statements, see Chapter 15, "Financial Statements," in *Start-Up Basics*.)

However, there is more to effective financial control than just generating financial statements. You will need to develop a good accounting and record-keeping system and to maintain good cash flow. These topics are covered in Chapters 14 through 16 in *Start-Up Basics*. Because adequate cash flow is a frequent problem in the event planning industry, we'll say more about it now.

Bucking Up

Keeping enough money flowing into a business is a universal concern, but the problem can be especially thorny in an industry that requires the payment of vendor and site deposits often months before an event. Planner Lee J. Howard suggests three strategies for maintaining good cash flow:

1. *Start with plenty of cash reserves.* Make sure that the amount you estimated in Chapter 5 for the first six months of operation is realistic.

2. *Take deposits.* Because you must pay vendor and site deposits and also purchase supplies, you should require deposits from clients upon signing of contracts. Dallas planners Deborah Williams, Kim Quigley, and David Granger require a minimum 50 percent deposit, with the balance to be paid at the time of the event. The deposit for an event contracted with very little lead time may be closer to 75 percent. "You should never be in the business of financing someone's party," says Kim.

> **Tip...**
>
> **Smart Tip**
> Whenever possible, save money by bartering services with other business owners. You could provide planning help in exchange for brochure printing services or the creation of signage, to name only a couple of exam-

3. *Charge enough for your services.* Make a careful assessment of what you need to charge to turn a healthy profit.

We've discussed the first two strategies elsewhere, but the third requires further explanation. What, you may ask, does "enough" mean? Read on, because we'll tackle that issue next.

The Price Is Right

The goal in pricing a service is to mark up your labor and materials costs sufficiently to cover overhead expenses and generate an acceptable profit. First-time business owners often fail without realizing that they priced their services too low.

According to industry expert Dr. Joe Goldblatt, fees are typically determined by three factors:

1. *Market segment served.* Social events have a different fee structure than corporate events. In the social events industry, planners typically receive a fee for their services, plus a percentage of some or all vendor fees. The two income streams produce enough revenue for a profit. If you were to break down your event planning fee into an hourly charge, a social planner would, according to industry consultant and author Patty Sachs, make anywhere from $10 to $75 per hour, depending on experience, plus vendor commissions. In the corporate events industry, however, planners typically charge a fee for their services, plus a handling charge for each item they contract. For example, a planner buys flowers from a florist, marks them up (usually 15 percent) and charges that amount to the client. Another possibility is a flat fee, or "project fee," often used when the event is large and the corporation wants to be given a "not to exceed" figure. Whichever method is used, Sachs estimates an hourly rate for corporate planners of between $15 and $150, plus vendor commissions. As these hourly figures imply, profit margins are typically greater for corporate events than they are for social ones.

2. *Geographic location.* Fees are higher in the Northeast, for example, than in the Southeast. This difference reflects the variation in cost of living. In addition, areas of the country that have well-defined on- and off-seasons base their prices partly on the season involved.

3. *Experience and reputation of the event planner.* If you are just starting out in the industry, it is reasonable to charge less

> **Smart Tip** *Tip...*
>
> Controlling costs is easier than trying to predict what your revenue will be. Remember, small expenses add up. For example, why pay extra to have a postal company pick up your packages if you can take them there yourself? Once you look for additional ways to save money, you'll find them. And Benjamin Franklin was right: "A penny saved is a penny

for your planning services while you gain expertise.

How, you may ask, are the above-mentioned fees-for-service calculated? Event planners we interviewed price their fees-for-service (the total cost to the client) using a "cost-plus" method. They contract out the labor, supplies, and materials involved in producing an event and charge their clients about 10 percent to 20 percent of the total cost of the event, with 15 percent being a rough average.

A word of caution concerning this method of pricing. Ideally, the percentage you charge above cost should provide you with a sufficient amount to cover that event's share of your overhead, as well as produce a profit. Overhead comprises all the nonlabor, indirect expenses required to operate your business. In general, overhead will be anywhere between 4 percent and 6 percent of the total price of the event. Your

Bright Idea

Another way to make sure your business doesn't suffer from a lack of cash is to sell gift certificates toward your planning services. Satisfied customers might buy them, and they are an excellent way to introduce others to your services. Furthermore, gift certificates are money in the bank because people often wait months before cashing them in.

Healthy Choices

Here are some additional ways of ensuring a good cash flow for your business:

- ○ *Pay your company's bills on time, but do not pay early.* Keep your money in the bank as long as possible. The single exception to this rule applies if you have negotiated vendor discounts for early payment (see Chapter 6).
- ○ *Negotiate the latest possible payment of the balance of vendor bills.* Often vendors will give you 30 days after the event in which to pay, especially if you have a good working relationship with them. This means if you get paid on the day of the event, you have 30 days of "free money" before you have to pay your vendors. And if the client is slow in paying, you have a cushion.
- ○ *Make sure your invoices are clear, accurate, and timely.* Being timely means sending your invoices as soon as you sign a contract or complete an event. The difficulty of collecting an account increases in direct proportion to its age.
- ○ *Keep inventory and supplies to a minimum.* According to industry expert and author Robin A. Kring, excessive overhead and inventory costs can seriously affect cash flow.

actual overhead expenses may vary depending on your own market conditions. Should your overhead expenses be too high, you will have to raise your commission to maintain sufficient profit. By raising your commission, you could become less competitive. It's a good idea to closely control your overhead expenses so they don't become too high relative to the price of the event.

Adding Up the Costs

As we mentioned in the research section in Chapter 3, you have to know exactly what your clients want and what they can spend to achieve it before you can begin planning an event. Then you estimate how much it will cost to contract for labor and supplies, add your commission to this sum, and present the total fee for services to the client as an estimate. Make sure you have filled out the Event Design Worksheet" starting on page 36. Those client needs will dictate what particular expenses you (and ultimately the client) will incur for that event. Below are some possible per-event expenses:

- *Site rental.* Depending on the event, site rental fees can be considerable, nonexistent, or anywhere in between.

Smart Tip

Tip...

As an additional way to beef up your cash flow, consider requiring clients to pay your bill in three installments rather than two. The first is the deposit, the second is a progress payment, and the third is due at the event itself. Note that if you do this, you will still probably want to have clients pay a deposit of close to 50 percent.

Marking It Up

Event planner Joyce Barnes-Wolff notes that the rule in the industry is to charge, on average, a commission of between 10 percent and 15 percent, depending on what the event involves. She evaluates the amount of her time and energy spent on the event. "My Rolodex is worth something, but if my role is simply picking up the phone and making calls and showing up for an event, I don't think it rates that kind of coordination fee." But if the event is complicated and creativity is what matters, then 10 percent to 15 percent is "very fair," she says.

Industry markups vary widely, ranging from 100 percent and up. Markup rates depend mostly on overhead costs, but the health of the economy also affects them. In troubled economic times, markups (and therefore profit margins) will be lower.

▲

- *Vendors.* This category could include a caterer, bartender, decorator, florist, photographer, or any of the vendors discussed in Chapter 6.
- *Supplies.* Any supplies not provided by vendors or by the client will need to be purchased by your company. These items can include anything from food to potted trees to table candles.
- *Equipment rental.* You may need to rent audiovisual or lighting equipment.
- *Licenses and permits.* As mentioned in Chapter 4, some types of events require special permits or licenses (e.g., Fire Marshall's permit or a license to use a musical score).
- *Transportation and parking.* If the event requires you or your staff to travel or requires the provision of transport for attendees or speakers, there may be significant transportation costs involved. These can include anything from airfare to car mileage and gasoline allowances.
- *Service fees and gratuities.* Hiring temporary help (e.g., servers) for the event can be costly.
- *Speakers' fees.* Conferences and other educational or commemorative events often involve speakers.
- *Publicity and invitations.* Getting the word out can be expensive. A large event may be heavily advertised, but even smaller events might entail the use of fliers. Invitations are also frequently necessary.
- *Mailing and shipping.* If you are mailing out invitations or fliers, don't forget this expense. Some event planners even ship flowers.
- *Photocopying and preparation of registration materials.* Any handouts for attendees or photocopying of fliers falls under this category.
- *Research and evaluations.* Depending on the nature of your inquiries and whether clients will benefit from them, you may not want to charge clients for these expenditures.
- *Signage.* Any signs or banners designed for the event should be figured into your per-event expenses.

Once you know your client's needs and which of the above expenses you will incur in planning the event, you can prepare an estimate of the event cost and of the fee-for-service. First, find out the going rate by contacting three of each kind of vendor you will need. Do the same for suppliers. Don't forget that price is not everything; consider the quality offered. Then figure the costs for each category listed (and any others that might arise), add them up,

Beware!
Make sure you figure "hidden" expenses like shipping, mailing, and parking fees into the estimates you give clients. All these costs add up, and you don't want them eating into your profit margin.

and add a small amount for unforeseen expenses (you be the judge of how much, depending on the size of the event).

When you give an estimate to a client, you may want to present it in the form of an itemized list. Show each vendor or supplier separately, perhaps with a brief description of the services he or she is to provide, and list the price of each service. This strategy is helpful, among other things, for reminding clients that your company will receive only a small fraction of the total fee for services. Add all event expenses together, then figure your commission as a percentage of this event cost.

Suppose you are presenting your estimate for an event that costs $6,945 to produce. Let's also assume that you charge a commission of 15 percent, an industry average. After itemizing the event costs, you would add in your commission in this manner:

Event Cost (E): $6,945

Commission (C): (15% of $6,945) =

.15 × 6,945 = $1,042

Finally, add the event cost and your commission to produce the fee-for-service (S). This figure represents the final cost to the client.

Fee-for-Service (S) = Event cost + Commission =

$6,945 + $1,042 = $7,987

So the final cost to the client is $7,987.

Although you should strive for an accurate estimate, you may find that your final total differs from the initial estimate. For this reason, you should make it clear to your clients that your estimate of the total event cost is just that—an estimate. Make sure that this fact is stated clearly in your contract. The contract should also specify that the client is responsible for any additional charges. Ensuring that you do not exceed your estimate by an unreasonable amount is an important part of your responsibility to your client.

Even-Steven

We have cautioned you to make sure you have a substantial amount of operating capital, enough to last until you reach the break-even point. How, you may ask, do you calculate a break-even point for an event planning business? The following is a detailed example of such an analysis:

- *Determine your monthly fixed costs.* Fixed costs (F) are those that do not change, no matter how many events you plan (e.g., rent, utilities). You completed a worksheet of these costs in Chapter 5. For the purpose of this break-even example, let's assume that you have monthly fixed costs of $1,910. So F = $1,910.

- *Determine your variable costs.* Variable costs are the costs of putting on the event you produce (e.g., hiring vendors, renting a site). Variable costs combine to produce the "event cost" (E). In this case, E = $6,945.

Beware!
You must keep records to determine your tax liabilities. Regardless of the type of bookkeeping system you use, your records must be permanent, accurate, and complete, and they must clearly establish income, deductions, credits, employee information, and anything else specified by federal, state, and local regulations. You must keep complete and separate records for each business.

- *Figure out the fee for service (S).* We just did this in the pricing example. We used an average rate of 15 percent, multiplied it by the event cost (E), and produced a commission (C) of $1,042. We then added the commission to the event cost to produce the fee for service. S = $7,987.

- *Now use the break-even equation.* Break-even = F divided by C: In this equation, F = fixed expenses and C = commission. Inputting our data from the example above, we find: Break-even = $1,910 divided by $1,042 = 1.8 events.

According to this break-even analysis, you will need to plan about two $8,000 events per month to pay all expenses and start making a profit.

You and Your Taxes

Managing your finances includes keeping a careful eye on your tax liabilities. For a thorough discussion, consult Chapter 17, "Taxes," in *Start-Up Basics* and the IRS *Tax Guide for Small Business* (Publication 334). Briefly, these taxes include the following:

- *Sales taxes.* Sales taxes are levied by many cities and states at varying rates. Most provide specific exemptions for certain classes of merchandise or particular groups of customers. Service businesses are often exempt altogether. Contact your state and/or local revenue offices for information on the law in your area so you can adapt your bookkeeping to the appropriate requirements. Many of the entrepreneurs we spoke to have resale tax ID numbers for their companies. This number entitles a business to buy merchandise (e.g., flowers) tax-free and charge clients the sales tax.

- *Personal income taxes.* If you are a sole proprietor or partner, you will not receive a salary like an employee. Therefore, no income tax will be withheld from the money you take out of your business for personal use. Instead, you must estimate your personal tax liability and pay it in quarterly installments.

- *Corporate income taxes.* If your business is organized as a corporation, you must pay taxes on all profits.

In addition to paying your own taxes, as a business owner and employer you will be responsible for collecting employee state and federal taxes and remitting them to the proper agencies. *Start-Up Basics* provides information on all these types of taxes. If you are a sole proprietor and plan to hire an employee, call the IRS at (800) TAX-FORM and ask for a copy of Form SS-4. Also call your state tax agency.

If you are like most event planners, you will hire some individuals as independent contractors (e.g., vendors). According to the IRS definition, independent contractors are individuals who perform services for more than one firm, determine how the work is to be done, use their own tools, hire and pay their own employees, and work for a fee rather than a salary. If you hire independent contractors, you have to file an annual information return (Form 1099—Miscellaneous) to report payments totaling $600 or more made to any individual in the course of trade or business during the calendar year. If you do not file this form, you will be subject to penalties. Be sure your records list the name, address, and Social Security number of every independent contractor you hired, along with pertinent dates and the amounts paid to each person. Every payment should be supported by an invoice from the contractor. Be warned also that if the IRS feels a worker whom you treated as a contractor should have been treated as an employee, you will be liable for payroll taxes that should have been withheld and paid, plus penalties and interest.

Working It Out

Good tax planning not only minimizes your taxes, but provides more money for your business. As an entrepreneur, you should view tax savings as a potential source of working capital. There are a few important rules to follow in your tax planning:

- *Don't incur an additional expense solely for the sake of getting an extra deduction.* This strategy is not cost-effective.
- *Immediately deferring taxes allows you to use your money interest-free before paying it to the government.* Interest rates may justify deferring taxes, though doing so may cost you more taxes in a later year.
- *If possible, claim income in the most advantageous year.* If, as you begin your business, you are employed by someone else and expect to receive a year-end bonus or other additional compensation, you may want to defer receipt until the forthcoming year, especially if you will be in a lower tax bracket at that time (e.g., perhaps quitting your job to devote full time to your business).

Spare the Expense

As an event planner, you may be able to deduct for the following types of expenses:

- *Home office*. You can deduct for all normal office expenses plus interest, taxes, insurance, and depreciation on the portion of your home that you use exclusively for business. To deduct, however, you must satisfy the following four usage criteria: Exclusive use (the space is not used for anything else), regular use (occasional use doesn't qualify), business use (you must conduct business, see clients, etc., in that space), and administrative use (you must handle administrative tasks at that location). Be aware that the IRS audits a high percentage of taxpayers with home offices.

- *Computers*. A home computer used exclusively for business may qualify for appropriate business deductions or credits.

- *Automobiles*. Depending on which method you use, you may deduct for mileage or for mileage plus depreciation, garage rent, insurance, and repairs, among other expenses.

- *Travel*. You must stay overnight on business to claim deductions on air, bus, or auto fares, hotel bills, and incidentals like dry cleaning and gratuities.

- *Entertainment*. You can deduct 50 percent of your expenses, but you must maintain records of the following: amount of expenditure; date of expenditure; name, address and type of entertainment; occupation of the person entertained; reason for entertainment; and the nature of the business discussion that took place (general goodwill is not accepted by the IRS). Rules for deductions change frequently. Keep up to date on them by ordering a current copy of the IRS Publication 535, *Business Expenses*. You can also look online at www.irs.gov.

- *Conferences and seminars*. The cost of the actual seminar is deductible, but deductions are no longer permitted for many of the expenses (e.g. food, lodging) incurred in connection with a conference, convention, or seminar.

- *Dues and subscriptions*. You may deduct these as long as they pertain to your field of business.

With proper management of your company's financial resources, you can greatly increase the probability that your business will succeed. In the next chapter, we'll discuss more ways you can ensure the success of your business.

Smart Tip

The year's end is the time to buy business equipment. You will get the same deduction whether you buy and use the equipment at the beginning or the end of the

Beware!

Make sure you do not make a mistake about what is tax-deductible. Penalty rates are high.

"I Came,
I Planned,
I Conquered"

This chapter has two topics: failure and success. Because we want to quickly move on to the more cheerful, optimistic topic, we'll first take a swift pass at ways to avoid failure.

Avoiding a Capsize

We're guessing that what you've read in earlier chapters has already given you an idea of the potential glitches of event planning. If you want to give yourself a little test, put down this book, make a list, and then compare it with ours. (If you feel your test-taking days are over, no problem. Just read on.) Here are some of the pitfalls specific to the event planning industry:

- *Misunderstanding your client's requirements.* If your client wants a conservative business meeting and you deliver a Roaring Twenties theme party, you're in trouble. Although this is an extreme example, remember that you need to know all your client's requirements in detail before you can arrange a successful event.

- *Poor choice of vendors or site.* Do your homework. Contract with reliable, reputable vendors who can meet your client's needs exactly. If your caterer serves a terrible meal, it's the caterer's fault that he or she can't cook. However, you're the one who made the hiring decision, so you'll take the blame. The buck stops with you. Be sure you can count on your vendors.

- *Lack of coordination between you and your team.* This is a related pitfall. Make sure you have a cooperative, "well-oiled" team (employees, vendors, and temporary staff) around you, and that everyone understands their respective roles in the production of the event.

- *Inaccurate estimates.* Your estimates should be as accurate as possible. If events go far over budget, your clients may end up having to pay more money than they can afford. If, on the other hand, you consistently come in at or below your estimates, you will probably have satisfied clients who will gladly recommend you to others.

- *Inadequate control of costs.* Take every reasonable opportunity to save. Pay attention to where money goes.

- *Poor cash flow.* In Chapter 8 we discussed ways to avoid this problem. One of the most effective is to require client deposits.

- *Inadequate insurance.* Make sure that you carry enough insurance to protect yourself in case anything goes wrong at an event. The planners that we spoke to carry about $1 million of liability insurance. If you don't have enough of the proper insurance, and if you're involved in a lawsuit, you could end up in bankruptcy.

> ## Bright Idea
> Everyone deserves recognition for a job well done. Recognizing employees who go above and beyond the call of duty can help keep your team "well-oiled." We all enjoy being rewarded, however small the token. Don't forget to reward yourself, too!

- *Poor customer service.* Much of what we covered in Chapter 7 can be encapsulated into one piece of advice: Make the event right. This is a golden rule in the event planning industry.

So how did you do? Now that you know some of the problems that can undermine an event planning business, be alert for any danger signs. If you react quickly enough, you can prevent financial disaster from striking. Ideally, of course, you will not merely react to threats, but instead anticipate changes, whether in the event planning field itself, in your clients' demands, or in the financial state of your business.

Smoothing Troubled Waters

You cannot anticipate every scenario, but it's important to plan for possible large-impact scenarios like inclement weather or security-related emergencies. Before the event, take a few moments to think through "what-ifs" and plan crisis management strategies with your staff. Make sure you know—and have readily available—the facility's emergency and security procedures. Also make sure personnel trained in CPR and other emergency procedures are present at the event.

Occasionally, in spite of your best efforts and meticulous planning, something goes wrong during an event. At that point, your biggest challenge may be to remain calm in the crisis and to think on your feet. However, if you're imagining disaster lurking around every corner, out of your control and waiting to trip you up, take heart. Because, in fact, much of effective troubleshooting is within your control and consists simply of making adequate preparations. In other words, in many cases good troubleshooting is proactive rather than reactive. Try to anticipate where problems might arise and plan for them. This strategy can be as simple as having backups for resources that are critical to an event's success.

Planner Martin Van Keken's firm produced a huge event on closing night of the Royal Ballet in Vancouver, British Columbia. Held outside at the Queen Elizabeth Theatre, the event's decor featured a spectacular English garden. Foreign dignitaries, including Margaret Thatcher and Princess Margaret, were in attendance. The evening event required a generator to supply power, and just before the guests were to enter the tented area, the generator failed. "It could not have happened at a worse moment," says Van Keken. Fortunately, they had a backup generator, although hooking it up took time. "A very long 5 or 10 minutes" after the guests entered the tented area, the lights came on, revealing the English

Profile

Kim Quigley makes sure her company doesn't rely exclusively on computers. She keeps a Rolodex, blank invoice slips, and a cash receipt book on hand in case of power outages or other computer problems. "I'm not shutting my doors because of a rainstorm," she says.

garden decor. And the guests applauded. "They all thought it was choreographed that way," says Martin. His story has a happy ending, but only because his company had the vital backup system.

Sometimes good troubleshooting involves persistence and a refusal to give up. Atlanta planner Lee J. Howard tells a story of a power failure in a building during one of his company's events. The building manager, who was responsible for backup power, said it wasn't working either and that there was no way to get help until Monday. "Meanwhile, we had a live band and 200 dancers on the floor." After examining the possibilities, they decided to try all the electrical outlets close to the stage. One in the men's room worked, and they had ampli-

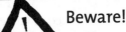

Beware!

With event planning, you don't have a second chance. If an event goes wrong, you can't tell the client to come back the next night. Keep yourself sane, however, by remembering that "There's no such thing as the perfect event," as Martin Van Keken puts it. Some event elements will be beyond your control. Be flexible and ready to think on your feet.

fied music back on within 15 minutes. "Although it was July and there was no AC or power for anything else, the party carried on successfully," he says. "The bottom line is, we took responsibility and didn't give up."

Jaclyn Bernstein didn't give up, either. Not even when disaster struck on 9-11. Her New York City company, Empire Force Events, was greatly affected by the tragedy. "We knew people who perished that day," she says. One of her employees lost her home, which was only a block from the twin towers. And, of course, tourism—and special events—in New York City nearly ground to a halt.

Her company responded in several ways. Empire Force Events took out photo ads in industry publications. The ads showed their team standing in front of the New York skyline. "It was a statement kind of advertising," she says, and it let people know they were still there. Her company also sent humorous e-mails to existing clients. One was a fake press release announcing that Empire Force Events would be adding Sea Mon-

keys to its staff in a bid to lower business costs. Another announced plans to auction off employees on eBay.

Empire Force Events also participated in a meeting and event coalition to bring business back to New York. "We took opportunities to be sponsors at major conventions in the industry," Bernstein adds.

Remember the best way to deal with unforeseen circumstances you cannot control is to remain as flexible as possible and be willing to try new strategies.

Bright Idea

As we have mentioned, planning and supervising events can be stressful. Give yourself and your company a break by taking steps to deal with stress. Take time out for activities you enjoy. Remember to allow time for friends and family, too.

Keeping the Boat Afloat

Besides being a good troubleshooter, what strategies can you adopt to give your event planning business the best possible chance for success? The planners and industry experts we interviewed provided the following advice:

- *Acquire professional training.* Says industry expert Dr. Joe Goldblatt, "The shortest route between exploring and succeeding in this profession is affiliation with a well-known school or university." Industry expert John Daly also recommends formal training.

- *Provide the service you say you will.* Use written contracts and stick to them. "And keep good records," suggests New York planner Jaclyn Bernstein.

- *Concentrate on the type of planning you do best.* "Don't try to do it all," advises industry expert and author Robin A. Kring.

- *Create a reliable team around you.* All planners mentioned the importance of staffing and vendor choices. "You design an event on paper," says Martin Van Keken. "Then you rely on other people."

- *Walk through the event.* Event planner Joyce Barnes-Wolff always does a mental walk-through: "In my mind I'm there. Do I have enough time? Are the press kits there?"

An Educational Experience

If you decide to get formal training in special events, there are several avenues you can explore. Consider courses in event management through a program such as the one at George Washington University in Washington, DC. Goldblatt, founder of the program, says that it offers both a master's degree and a certificate program. Certification requires a minimum of seven courses and takes two years to complete. Courses are offered on campus, in five other cities, and through distance learning (i.e., via the Internet). For more information, consult the program's Web site at www.gwu.edu.

The International Special Events Society (ISES) Conference for Professional Development (CPD) is a series of professional seminars focusing on the latest trends and developments in the special events industry. Offered through ISES, this conference offers both educational and networking opportunities.

As previously mentioned, The Special Event also offers you a chance to learn as you network. Held annually in January, this prestigious industry trade show is put on by Primedia Business Magazine & Media Inc., which also publishes *Special Events Magazine*. For contact information on any of these sources, consult the Appendix.

- *Keep your cool.* "Keep your focus," says Dallas planner David Granger. "Try to be one step ahead," suggests Martin Van Keken. "Getting upset doesn't help," he adds.

- *Expect the unexpected.* Many event planners mentioned this one. "There's always something that will go differently than planned," says Van Keken. Not necessarily wrong, he stresses, but differently. "You've got to be ready for that."

- *Be ready with Plan B.* This is closely related to the last piece of advice. "I never do an outdoor event without a rain plan," says Barnes-Wolff.

- *Make your clients happy.* As we have stated, this is a golden rule in event planning. "In this industry there is no right or wrong except to make the client happy," says Granger. Doing the work and getting it right is what matters, agrees Bernstein.

Smooth Sailing

Developing a strong customer base, paying close attention to clients' needs, finding a niche, and coping with a changing economy are all proven ways to keep a business successful and out of financial difficulty. Remember, periodically ask yourself the following questions:

- Have I carefully analyzed the demand for my services, monitored the marketplace, and adjusted to changing conditions?

- Have I found a niche that provides me with enough events to plan, without involving too wide a range?

- Do I have an accurate and realistic amount of cash reserves?

- Do I have a business plan and mission statement?

- Are my services priced accurately?

- Have I kept my overhead costs to an absolute minimum?

- Have I created a good team, with well-chosen staff and vendors?

- Does my company provide the kind of customer service that keeps clients coming back?

If you answered "yes" to all these questions, congratulations! Your company has an excellent chance of success. If you had any "no" answers, these are the areas that need work. And identifying these areas puts you in a good position to make the corrections that will create a thriving business.

Event planning is a "happy" industry. You have chosen a field that will allow you to create wonderful memories for many people. If you do just that, success will follow. So go out there and have fun!

And celebrate!

Appendix
Event Planning Resources

The Duchess of Windsor famously said that you can never be too rich or too thin. While that could be argued, it's true that you can never have too many resources. Therefore, for your consideration, here is a wealth of sources to investigate as you develop your plans for establishing an event planning business.

These sources are only the beginning. They are by no means the only sources available to you, nor can any claim total authority. Event planning is a volatile field, and businesses tend to move, change, fold, and expand. It's up to you to do your homework. Get out and start asking questions.

An extra word of advice: We strongly suggest you surf the Net for information. So long as you confirm your sources, you'll find abundant information about business trends on the Net, as well as related associations, books, conferences, and software.

Associations

American Society of Association Executives, 1575 I St. NW, Washington, DC 20005-1103, (202) 626-2723, www.asaenet.org

Convention Industry Council, 8201 Greensboro Dr., #300, McLean, VA 22102, (703) 610-9030, www.conventionindustry.org

International Association of Convention & Visitors Bureaus, 2025 M St. NW, #500, Washington, DC 20036, (202) 296-7888, www.iacvb.org

International Festivals & Events Association, 2601 Eastover Terrace, Boise, ID 83706, (208) 433-0950, www.ifea.com

International Special Events Society, 401 N. Michigan Ave., Chicago, IL 60611, (800) 688-4737, www.ises.com

Meeting Professionals International, 4455 LBJ Fwy., #1200, Dallas, TX 75244-5903, (972) 702-3000, www.mpiweb.org

National Association of Catering Executives, 5565 Sterrett Pl., #328, Columbia, MD 21044, (410) 997-9055, www.nace.net

Professional Convention Management Association, 2301 S. Lake Shore Dr., #1001, Chicago, IL 60616-1419, (312) 423-7262, www.pcma.org

Books

The Art of Event Design, Liese Gardner and Susan Terpening, Primedia Business Magazines & Media Inc., 23805 Stuart Ranch Rd., Malibu, CA 90265, (800) 543-4116

Behind the Scenes at Special Events: Flowers, Props and Design, Lena Malouf, John Wiley & Sons, www.wiley.com

Big Meetings, Big Results, Tom McMahon Meeting Professionals International, 4455 LBJ Fwy., #1200, Dallas, TX 75244-5903, (972) 702-3044, www.mpiweb.org

The Business of Event Planning: Behind-the-Scenes Secrets of Successful Special Events, Judy Allen, John Wiley & Sons Inc., www.wiley.com

CIC Manual, Convention Industry Council, 8201 Greensboro Dr., #300, McLean, VA 22102, (703) 610-9030, www.conventionindustry.org

The Complete Idiot's Guide to Throwing a Great Party, Phyllis Cambria and Patty Sachs, Alpha Books, www.idiotsguides.com

Creating Special Events: The Ultimate Guide to Producing Successful Events, L. Surbeck, Master Publications, 10331 Linn Station Rd., Louisville, KY 40223, (502) 426-6673

Dollars and Events: How to Succeed in the Special Events Business, J. Goldblatt and C. McKibben, John Wiley & Sons, www.wiley.com

Event Planning: The Ultimate Guide to Successful Meetings, Corporate Events, Fundraising Galas, Conferences, Conventions, Incentives and Other Special Events, Judy Allen, John Wiley & Sons, www.wiley.com

The International Dictionary of Event Management, J. Goldblatt and C. McKibben, John Wiley & Sons, www.wiley.com

ISES Gold, International Special Events Society, 401 N. Michigan Ave., Chicago, IL 60611, (800) 688-4737, www.ises.com

Pick a Party: The Big Book of Party Menus, Recipes and Table Decor, Patty Sachs, Meadowbrook Press, 5451 Smetana Dr., Minnetonka, MN 55343, (952) 930-1100, www.meadowbrookpress.com

Pick a Party: The Big Book of Party Themes and Occasions, Patty Sachs, Meadowbrook Press, 5451 Smetana Dr., Minnetonka, MN 55343, (952) 930-1100, fax: (952) 930-1940, www.meadowbrookpress.com

Reunions for Fun-Loving Families, N. F. Bagley, Brighton Publications Inc., P.O. Box 120706, St. Paul, MN 55112, (800) 536-2665, www.partybooks.com

The Special Event Risk Management Manual, Alexander Berlonghi, International Special Events Society, 401 N. Michigan Ave., Chicago, IL 60611, (800) 688-4737

Special Events: The Art and Science of Celebration, Dr. Joe Goldblatt, 401 N. Michigan Ave., Chicago, IL 60611, (800) 688-4737

Special Events: Global Event Management in the 21st Century, Dr. Joe Goldblatt, John Wiley & Sons Inc., www.wiley.com

Themes, Dreams and Schemes: Banquet Menu Ideas, Concepts and Thematic Experiences, G. Eugene Wigger, John Wiley & Sons, www.wiley.com

Educational Opportunities

Alan Shawn Feinstein Graduate School, offers the first MBA concentration in Event Leadership, Johnson & Wales University, 8 Abbott Park Pl., Providence, RI 02903, (401) 598-4760, www.jwu.edu

Convention Industry Council, offers training to become a Certified Meeting Professional, 8201 Greensboro Dr., #300, McLean, VA 22102, (703) 610-9030, www.conventionindustry.org

The George Washington University International Institute of Tourism Studies, offers both a master's degree and a certificate program in event management, 600 21st St. NW, Washington, DC 20007, (202) 994-6281, www.gwu.edu

International Special Events Society, provides certification as a Certified Special Events Professional, 401 N. Michigan Ave., Chicago, IL 60611, (800) 688-4737, www.ises.com

Event Planning Software

CEO Software Inc. (Optimum Settings II, Scheduler Plus, Scheduler Plus II), 2231 N. Indian Ruins Rd., Tucson, AZ 85715, (520) 296-7577, www.optimumsettings.com

Certain Software (Meeting Planner Plus, Register 123), One Daniel Burnham Ct., #330C, San Francisco, CA 94109, (888) CERTAIN, www.certain.com

EKEBA International (Complete Event Manager), P.O. Box 15131, Columbus, OH 43215-0131, (800) 847-4561, www.ekeba.com

EventPro Software (EventPro, Event Planner), #105-15 Innovation Bl., Saskatoon, SK, CAN S7N 2XB, (306) 975-3737, www.eventpro.net

Gomembers (MeetingTrak, MemberTrak, VendorTrak), 11720 Sunrise Valley Dr., #300, Reston, VA 20191, (800) 779-7430, www.gomembers.com

PC/Nametag (PC/Nametag PRO II), 124 Horizon Dr., Verona, WI 53593, (800) 233-9767, www.pcnametag.com

TimeSaver Software (Room Viewer), 17731 Irvine Bl., #201-A, Tustin, CA 92780, (714) 731-5390, www.timesaversoftware.com

Industry Experts

John Daly Jr., CSEP, John Daly Inc., 8 E. Arrellaga St., Santa Barbara, CA 93101, (805) 963-5007, www.jdalyinc.com

Dr. Joe Goldblatt, CSEP, Dean, Alan Shawn Feinstein Graduate School, Johnson & Wales University, 8 Abbott Park Pl., Providence, RI 02903, (401) 598-4760, www.jwu.edu

Patty Sachs, author and presenter (with Phyllis Cambria) of the "Getting Started Tele-Seminars Series," www.partyplansplus.com

Magazines and Publications

Corporate & Incentive Travel, Coastal Communications, 2650 N. Military Trail, #250, Boca Raton, FL 33431-6309, (561) 989-0600, www.corporate-inc-travel.com

Event Solutions Magazine, Event Publishing LLC, 5400 S. Lakeshore Dr., #101, Tempe, AZ 85283, (480) 831-5100, www.event-solutions.com

The Meeting Professional, 4455 LBJ Fwy., #1200, Dallas, TX 75244-5903, (972) 702-3000, www.mpiweb.org

Meetings & Conventions, NorthStar Travel Media, 500 Plaza Dr., Secaucus, NJ 07094-3626, (201) 902-1700, www.meetings-conventions.com

Special Events Magazine, Primedia Business Magazines & Media Inc, 23805 Stuart Ranch Rd., Malibu, CA 90265, (800) 543-4116

Successful Meetings, Bill Communications Inc., 770 Broadway, New York, NY 10003, (646) 654-4500, www.billcom.com

Tradeshow Week, Tradeshow Week, 5700 Wilshire Bl., #120, Los Angeles, CA 90036, (323) 965-2437, www.tradeshowweek.com

Travel Weekly, NorthStar Travel Media, 500 Plaza Dr., Secaucus, NJ 07094-3626, (201) 902-1700, www.travelweekly.com

Online Event Planning Forums/Web Sites

www.alltimefavorites.com (All Time Favorites Inc.), a good site for searching for vendors and getting proposals

www.bizbash.com (BizBash.com), a trendy site, featuring lots of ideas for events

www.conworld.net (Conworld.net), contains, among other things, a list of event planning software

www.dmoz.org (Open Directory Project), the hospitality software section in the business area features a long list of software sites for event planning

www.event-planner.com (Event Planner), provides many useful resources

www.eventplanner.com (EventPlanner.com), more resources

www.eventplanning.net (The Event Planning Network), find suppliers, planning tips, chat and discussion areas, etc.

www.expoworld.net (Sponsored by Las Vegas Convention and Visitors Authority), offers many event sites, publications, directories, and articles

www.ezeventplanner.com (EZEventPlanner), use this site to help you plan your entire event

www.ises.com (International Special Events Society), an association of more than 3,000 special events professionals, 30 percent of whom are event planners; Web site features information on joining ISES, a forum for networking with event planners and others in the special events industry, an online copy of ISES' code of ethics, information on local chapters, and more

www.meetings-conventions.com (Meetings & Conventions Online), contains news and feature stories from the latest issue of *Meetings & Conventions* magazine, an events calendar, directory of previously published articles (which have to be ordered separately), plus links to conventions and visitors bureaus throughout the United States

▲

www.mpiweb.org (Meeting Professionals International), an organization of more than 14,000 meeting planners for the corporate market (some of whom are independent planners) supports this Web site consisting mainly of membership information and benefits; you'll also find a database of MPI suppliers, an online version of its bookstore catalog, and local chapter information

www.partyplansplus.com (PartyPlansPlus.com), site provides event ideas, advice, newsletters, and other great resources for event planners

www.pattysachs.com (Party-Planning By Patti Sachs), the "Super Disk Deal," by Patty Sachs and Dawn Hogan, offers 52 reports and forms for event and party planners

www.seatingarrangement.com (SeatingArrangement), plan your seating using information from this site

www.specialeventsite.com (SpecialEventSite), search for many different types of sites

Successful Event Planners

Designs Behind the Scenes Inc., Deborah K. Williams, Kim I. Quigley, David Granger, 2809 Canton St., Dallas, TX 75226, (214) 747-1904, www.dbtsinc.com

Empire Force Events Inc., Jaclyn Bernstein, DMCP, 71 West 23rd St., 6th Fl., New York, NY 10010-4102, (212) 924-0320, www.empireforce.com

JBW Productions, Joyce Barnes-Wolff, 17 South High St., #640, Columbus, OH 43215, (614) 233-3320, www.jbwProductions.com

Lee J. Howard Entertainment Inc., Lee J. Howard, 1146 Green St., #6, Roswell, GA 30075, (770) 643-6001, www.leejhoward.com

MVKA Productions, Martin Van Keken, 3A-138 West Sixth Ave., Vancouver, BC, CAN V5Y 1K6, (604) 708-0085, www.mvka.com

Glossary

Actualization: an accounting of an event planning business's expenditures (both time and money) in producing an event

American Society of Association Executives (ASAE): an organization for association executives

Bond: an insurance contract used by service companies as a guarantee that they have the necessary ability and financial backing to meet their obligations

Break-even point: the point at which your company neither makes nor loses money

Caterer: a company retained to provide food (and usually beverages, too) for an event

Contingency plan: a written plan that is prepared in advance to address possible emergencies

Contractor: an individual or a company under contract to provide goods or services

Convention and visitors bureau: nonprofit organizations that provides products and services to planners

Copyright: a form of protection used to safeguard original literary works, performing arts, sound recordings, and visual arts

▲

Corporate planner: an individual who plans meetings for companies

Destination management company (DMC): a business that handles entertainment for a group of individuals (often conference or meeting attendees) from out of town

Evaluation: written feedback about an event from attendees or other parties

Indemnification: a legal term meaning one party agrees to protect the other party from liability or damages related to an event

International Special Events Society (ISES): the largest association for special events professionals

Invoice: a document that indicates costs for goods or services owed by one individual or company to another

Liability: the legal responsibility for an act, especially as pertaining to insurance risks

Markup: the amount added to the cost of goods or services to produce the desired profit

Meeting professional: an individual who plans and provides services for meetings, conferences, etc.

Meeting Professionals International (MPI): the largest association for meeting professionals

Proposal: a document outlining what a business will do for a client and the price at which it will be done

Relational database: a set of data structured so that information can be accessed across different databases

Site: the location for an event

Supplier: the individual or company that sells goods or services to another company; term often used synonymously with "vendor"

Target market: the section of the market, or group of people, to whom a company hopes to sell its product

Vendor: the company retained by an event planner to handle one or more aspects of an event; term sometimes used synonymously with "supplier"

Vendor agreement: a legal contract between event planner and vendor

Venue: a site for an event

Index